You Can Hear the Ocean

An Anthology of Classic and Current Poetry

Edited by
Gene Hult

Brighten Press

Houston

Copyright © 2019 by Brighten Press

All rights reserved. This book or any portion thereof may not be reproduced or used in any manner or media without the permission of the publisher or author except for the use of brief quotations in a book review or academic essay.

First Edition, 2019

ISBN 978-1-7323381-8-0 (paperback)
ISBN 978-1-7323381-9-7 (ebook)

Brighten Press
Houston, Texas

info@brightenpress.com
www.brightenpress.com

Cover photo by Citysqwirl.

You Can Hear the Ocean

Contents

Classic — 1

Eugene Lee-Hamilton — 3
Sea-Shell Murmurs

Marianne Moore — 4
A Talisman

Ezra Pound — 5
The Sea of Glass

Oscar Wilde — 6
Impression du Voyage

Alan Seeger — 7
On the Cliffs, Newport

Sadakichi Hartmann — 8
Drifting Flowers of the Sea

Edna St. Vincent Millay — 9
Low-Tide

H. D. — 10
Sea Iris

Joseph Auslander — 11
I Know It Will Be Quiet When You Come

Wallace Stevens — 12
The Paltry Nude Starts on a Spring Voyage

John Masefield — 13
Sea Fever

Thomas Hardy 14
The Convergence of the Twain

Marianne Moore 16
A Jelly-Fish

Rudyard Kipling 17
Seal Lullaby

Walt Whitman 18
Out of the Rolling Ocean, the Crowd

Emily Dickinson 19
I Started Early—Took My Dog—

A. E. 20
The Voice of the Sea

William Shakespeare 21
Sonnet LXIV

Elizabeth Barrett Browning 22
A Sea-Side Walk

William Butler Yeats 24
The White Birds

Stephen Crane 25
The Ocean Said to Me Once

Thomas Moore 26
The Fire Worshippers

Dante Alighieri 27
The Sailing of Ulysses

Alfred, Lord Tennyson 30
On a Desert Island

Henry Wadsworth Longfellow 32
Seaweed

Thomas Lovell Beddoes *To Sea, to Sea!*	34
George Shepard Burleigh *An Ocean Sunrise*	35
Ralph Waldo Emerson *Seashore*	36
John Boyle O'Reilly *The Flying Dutchman*	38
Charlotte Perkins Gilman *The Rock and the Sea*	46
Emily Dickinson *I Think that the Root of the Wind Is Water—*	49
Rainer Maria Rilke *Song of the Sea*	50
Nathaniel Hawthorne *The Ocean*	51
Sara Teasdale *Sea Longing*	52
Lord Byron *The Ocean*	53
Dante Gabriel Rossetti *The Sea-Limits*	56
D. H. Lawrence *The Mystic Blue*	58
Arthur Guiterman *A Sea Dream*	59
Emily Dickinson *Exultation Is the Going*	60

Thomas S. Jones, Jr. 61
Dusk at Sea

John Sterling 62
The Two Oceans

Bliss Carman 63
A Son of the Sea

Robert Louis Stevenson 64
A Visit from the Sea

Elizabeth Barrett Browning 65
The Sea-Mew

Eva L. Ogden 67
The Sea

Edna St. Vincent Millay 68
Exiled

William Wordsworth 70
The Sea Shell

Current 71

Jenny Blackford 73
The Way the Water

Ben Bever 75
Sea-glass

David Holper 76
To Pewetole Island

Carol Alena Aronoff 78
The Muse

Joel Allegretti   79
The Sea at Our Door

Janet Barry   80
wrack line

Elizabeth Ruth Deyro   82
Let the Oceans Speak for Me

Gene Hult   83
Sea Stack

Paul Magrs   85
Across the Ocean

Lynne Viti   87
Lament

Suzanne S. Rancourt   89
The Shores of Methana

Lucinda Marshall   91
Ebb Tide

Alec Solomita   92
Familiar

Joel Allegretti   93
Gabriel the Beachcomber

R. T. Castleberry   95
The Mission of Water

Bill Cushing   96
Sailing

Ciarán Parkes   97
Kelp

Lauren Davis   98
Land Not Required

Agnieszka Filipek — 99
Mermaid

Larry D. Thacker — 100
Fisherman's Runes

Sidney Bending — 101
Dead Zones, Dying Zones

Alison Stone — 102
The Sea

Leah Mueller — 104
At the Memorial

Meg Smith — 107
Seafoam Witch

Marj Hahne — 108
Hold Fast

Clarissa Jakobsons — 110
California Ohms

Gene Hult — 111
Seizure

Stephen McGuinness — 115
Parallel

Eloise Bruce — 116
Having Uncles Named Homer

Marjorie Maddox — 118
Sea Side Be

Alec Solomita — 119
Another Poem about the Sea

Winston Plowes — 120
Orcadian

About the Authors — 121

Acknowledgments — 137

Reading Guide — 139

Classic

Eugene Lee-Hamilton

Sea-Shell Murmurs

The hollow sea-shell, which for years hath stood
On dusty shelves, when held against the ear
Proclaims its stormy parents; and we hear
The faint far murmur of the breaking flood.
We hear the sea. The sea? It is the blood
In our own veins, impetuous and near,
And pulses keeping pace with hope and fear
And with our feelings' every shifting mood.
Lo, in my heart I hear, as in a shell,
The murmur of a world beyond the grave,
Distinct, distinct, though faint and far it be.
Thou fool; this echo is a cheat as well,—
The hum of earthly instincts; and we crave
A world unreal as the shell-heard sea.

Marianne Moore

A Talisman

Under a splintered mast,
torn from ship and cast
near her hull,

a stumbling shepherd found
embedded in the ground,
a sea-gull

of lapis lazuli,
a scarab of the sea,
with wings spread—

curling its coral feet,
parting its beak to greet
men long dead.

Ezra Pound

The Sea of Glass

I looked and saw a sea
        roofed over with rainbows,
In the midst of each
        two lovers met and departed;
Then the sky was full of faces
        with gold glories behind them.

Oscar Wilde

Impression du Voyage

The sea was sapphire colored, and the sky
  Burned like a heated opal through air,
  We hoisted sail; the wind was blowing fair
For the blue lands that to the eastward lie.
From the steep prow I marked with quickening eye
  Zakynthos, every olive grove and creek,
  Ithaca's cliff, Lycaon's snowy peak,
And all the flower-strewn hills of Arcady.
The flapping of the sail against the mast,
  The ripple of the water on the side,
  The ripple of girls' laughter at the stern,
The only sounds:—when 'gan the West to burn,
  And a red sun upon the seas to ride,
  I stood upon the soil of Greece at last!

Alan Seeger

On the Cliffs, Newport

Tonight a shimmer of gold lies mantled o'er
Smooth lovely Ocean. Through the lustrous gloom
A savor steals from linden trees in bloom
And gardens ranged at many a palace door.
Proud walls rise here, and, where the moonbeams pour
Their pale enchantment down the dim coast-line,
Terrace and lawn, trim hedge and flowering vine,
Crown with fair culture all the sounding shore.
How sweet, to such a place, on such a night,
From halls with beauty and festival a-glare,
To come distract and, stretched on the cool turf,
Yield to some fond, improbable delight,
While the moon, reddening, sinks, and all the air
Sighs with the muffled tumult of the surf!

Sadakichi Hartmann

Drifting Flowers of the Sea

Across the dunes, in the waning light,
The rising moon pours her amber rays,
Through the slumbrous air of the dim, brown night
The pungent smell of the seaweed strays—
  From vast and trackless spaces
    Where wind and water meet,
      White flowers, that rise from the sleepless deep,
        Come drifting to my feet.
  They flutter the shore in a drowsy tune,
    Unfurl their bloom to the lightlorn sky,
      Allow a caress to the rising moon,
        Then fall to slumber, and fade, and die.

White flowers, a-bloom on the vagrant deep,
Like dreams of love, rising out of sleep,
You are the songs, I dreamt but never sung,
Pale hopes my thoughts alone have known,
Vain words ne'er uttered, though on the tongue,
That winds to the sibilant seas have blown.
  In you, I see the everlasting drift of years
    That will endure all sorrows, smiles and tears;
      For when the bell of time will ring the doom
        To all the follies of the human race,
          You still will rise in fugitive bloom
            And garland the shores of ruined space.

Edna St. Vincent Millay

Low-Tide

These wet rocks where the tide has been,
  Barnacled white and weeded brown
And slimed beneath to a beautiful green,
  These wet rocks where the tide went down
Will show again when the tide is high
  Faint and perilous, far from shore,
No place to dream, but a place to die,—
  The bottom of the sea once more.

There was a child that wandered through
  A giant's empty house all day,—
House full of wonderful things and new,
  But no fit place for a child to play.

H. D.

Sea Iris

I.
Weed, moss-weed,
root tangled in sand,
sea-iris, brittle flower,
one petal like a shell
is broken,
and you print a shadow
like a thin twig.

Fortunate one,
scented and stinging,
rigid myrrh-bud,
camphor-flower,
sweet and salt—you are wind
in our nostrils.

II.
Do the murex-fishers
drench you as they pass?
Do your roots drag up colour
from the sand?
Have they slipped gold under you—
rivets of gold?

Band of iris-flowers
above the waves,
you are painted blue,
painted like a fresh prow
stained among the salt weeds.

Joseph Auslander

I Know It Will Be Quiet When You Come

I know it will be quiet when you come:
No wind; the water breathing steadily;
A light like ghost of silver on the sea;
And the surf dreamily fingering his drum.
Twilight will drift in large and leave me numb
With nearness to the last tranquility;
And then the slow and languorous tyranny
Of orange moon, pale night, and cricket hum.

And suddenly there will be twist of tide,
A rustling as of thin silk on the sand,
The tremor of a presence at my side,
The tremble of a hand upon my hand:
And pulses sharp with pain, and fires fanned,
And words that stumble into stars and hide.

Wallace Stevens

The Paltry Nude Starts on a Spring Voyage

But not on a shell, she starts,
Archaic, for the sea.
But on the first-found weed
She scuds the glitters,
Noiselessly, like one more wave.

She too is discontent
And would have purple stuff upon her arms,
Tired of the salty harbors,
Eager for the brine and bellowing
Of the high interiors of the sea.

The wind speeds her on,
Blowing upon her hands
And watery back.
She touches the clouds, where she goes,
In the circle of her traverse of the sea.

Yet this is meagre play
In the scrurry and water-shine,
As her heels foam—
Not as when the goldener nude
Of a later day

Will go, like the centre of sea-green pomp,
In an intenser calm,
Scullion of fate,
Across the spick torrent, ceaselessly,
Upon her irretrievable way.

John Masefield

Sea Fever

I must down to the seas again,
to the lonely sea and the sky,
And all I ask is a tall ship
and a star to steer her by;
And the wheel's kick and the wind's song
and the white sail's shaking,
And a grey mist on the sea's face,
and a grey dawn breaking.

I must down to the seas again,
for the call of the running tide
Is a wild call and a clear call
that may not be denied;
And all I ask is a windy day
with the white clouds flying,
And the flung spray and the blown spume,
and the sea-gulls crying.

I must down to the seas again,
to the vagrant gypsy life,
To the gull's way and the whale's way
where the wind's like a whetted knife;
And all I ask is a merry yarn
from a laughing fellow-rover,
And quiet sleep and a sweet dream
when the long trick's over.

Thomas Hardy

The Convergence of the Twain

(Lines on the loss of the "Titanic")

I.

>In a solitude of the sea
>Deep from human vanity,
>
>And the Pride of Life that planned her, stilly couches she.

II.

>Steel chambers, late the pyres
>Of her salamandrine fires,
>
>Cold currents thrid, and turn to rhythmic tidal lyres.

III.

>Over the mirrors meant
>To glass the opulent
>
>The sea-worm crawls—grotesque, slimed, dumb, indifferent.

IV.

>Jewels in joy designed
>To ravish the sensuous mind
>
>Lie lightless, all their sparkles bleared and black and blind.

V.

>Dim moon-eyed fishes near
>Gaze at the gilded gear
>
>And query: "What does this vaingloriousness down here. . . ?"

VI.
        Well: while was fashioning
        This creature of cleaving wing,
The Immanent Will that stirs and urges everything

VII.
        Prepared a sinister mate
        For her—so gaily great—
A Shape of Ice, for the time far and dissociate.

VIII.
        And as the smart ship grew
        In stature, grace, and hue,
In shadowy silent distance grew the Iceberg too.

IX.
        Alien they seemed to be:
        No mortal eye could see
The intimate welding of their later history,

X.
        Or sign that they were bent
        By paths coincident
On being anon twin halves of one august event,

XI.
        Till the Spinner of the Years
        Said "Now!" And each one hears,
And consummation comes, and jars two hemispheres.

Marianne Moore

A Jelly-Fish

Visible, invisible,
A fluctuating charm,
An amber-colored amethyst
Inhabits it; your arm
Approaches, and
It opens and
It closes;
You have meant
To catch it,
And it shrivels;
You abandon
Your intent—
It opens, and it
Closes and you
Reach for it—
The blue
Surrounding it
Grows cloudy, and
It floats away
From you.

Rudyard Kipling

Seal Lullaby

Oh! hush thee, my baby, the night is behind us,
  And black are the waters that sparkled so green.
The moon, o'er the combers, looks downward to find us
  At rest in the hollows that rustle between.
Where billow meets billow, there soft be thy pillow;
  Ah, weary wee flipperling, curl at thy ease!
The storm shall not wake thee, nor shark overtake thee,
  Asleep in the arms of the slow-swinging seas.

Walt Whitman

Out of the Rolling Ocean, the Crowd

1.
Out of the rolling ocean, the crowd,
came a drop gently to me,
Whispering, *I love you, before long I die,*
I have travel'd a long way, merely to look on you,
to touch you,
For I could not die till I once look'd on you,
For I fear'd I might afterward lose you.

2.
(Now we have met, we have look'd, we are safe;
Return in peace to the ocean, my love;
I too am part of that ocean, my love—
we are not so much separated;
Behold the great rondure—
the cohesion of all, how perfect!
But as for me, for you, the irresistible sea is to separate us,
As for an hour carrying us diverse—
yet cannot carry us diverse forever;
Be not impatient—a little space—know you,
I salute the air, the ocean and the land,
Every day, at sundown, for your dear sake, my love.)

Emily Dickinson

I Started Early—Took My Dog—

I started Early—Took my Dog—
And visited the Sea—
The Mermaids in the Basement
Came out to look at me—

And Frigates—in the Upper Floor
Extended Hempen Hands—
Presuming Me to be a Mouse—
Aground—upon the Sands—

But no Man Moved me—till the Tide
Went past my simple Shoe—
And past my Apron—and my Belt—
And past my Bodice—too—

And made as He would eat me up—
As wholly as a Dew
Upon a Dandelion's Sleeve—
And then—I started—too.

And He—He followed—close behind—
I felt His Silver Heel
Upon my Ankle,—Then My Shoes
Would overflow with Pearl—

Until We met the Solid Town—
No One He seemed to know—
And bowing—with a Mighty look—
At me—The Sea withdrew—

A. E.

The Voice of the Sea

The sea was hoary, hoary,
Beating on rock and cave:
The winds were white and weeping
With foam dust of the wave.

They thundered louder, louder,
With storm-lips curled in scorn—
And dost thou tremble before us,
O fallen star of morn?

William Shakespeare

Sonnet LXIV

When I have seen by Time's fell hand defaced
The rich proud cost of outworn buried age,
When sometime lofty towers I see down razed,
And brass eternal slave to mortal rage.
When I have seen the hungry ocean gain
Advantage on the kingdom of the shore,
And the firm soil win of the watery main,
Increasing store with loss, and loss with store.
When I have seen such interchange of state,
Or state itself confounded, to decay,
Ruin hath taught me thus to ruminate
That Time will come and take my love away.
  This thought is as a death which cannot choose
  But weep to have that which it fears to lose.

Elizabeth Barrett Browning

A Sea-Side Walk

I.

     We walked beside the sea,
After a day which perished silently
Of its own glory—like the Princess weird
Who, combating the Genius, scorched and seared,
Uttered with burning breath, "Ho! victory!"
And sank adown, an heap of ashes pale;
     So runs the Arab tale.

II.

     The sky above us showed
An universal and unmoving cloud,
On which, the cliffs permitted us to see
Only the outline of their majesty,
As master-minds, when gazed at by the crowd!
And, shining with a gloom, the water grey
     Swang in its moon-taught way.

III.

     Nor moon nor stars were out.
They did not dare to tread so soon about,
Though trembling, in the footsteps of the sun.
The light was neither night's nor day's, but one
Which, life-like, had a beauty in its doubt;
And Silence's impassioned breathings round
     Seemed wandering into sound.

IV.
> O solemn-beating heart
Of nature! I have knowledge that thou art
Bound unto man's by cords he cannot sever—
And, what time they are slackened by him ever,
So to attest his own supernal part,
Still runneth thy vibration fast and strong,
> The slackened cord along.

V.
> For though we never spoke
Of the grey water and the shaded rock,—
Dark wave and stone unconsciously, were fused
Into the plaintive speaking that we used,
Of absent friends and memories unforsook;
And, had we seen each other's face, we had
> Seen haply, each was sad.

William Butler Yeats

The White Birds

I would that we were, my beloved,
white birds on the foam of the sea!
We tire of the flame of the meteor,
before it can pass by and flee;
And the flame of the blue star of twilight,
hung low on the rim of the sky,
Has awaked in our hearts, my beloved,
a sadness that may not die.

A weariness comes from those dreamers,
dew dabbled, the lily and rose,
Ah, dream not of them, my beloved,
the flame of the meteor that goes,
Or the flame of the blue star that lingers
hung low in the fall of the dew:
For I would we were changed to white birds
on the wandering foam: I and you!

I am haunted by numberless islands,
and many a Danaan shore,
Where Time would surely forget us,
and Sorrow come near us no more;
Soon far from the rose and the lily,
and fret of the flames would we be,
Were we only white birds, my beloved,
buoyed out on the foam of the sea!

Stephen Crane

The Ocean Said to Me Once

The ocean said to me once,
"Look!
Yonder on the shore
Is a woman, weeping.
I have watched her.
Go you and tell her this,—
Her lover I have laid
In cool green hall.
There is wealth of golden sand
And pillars, coral-red;
Two white fish stand guard at his bier.

"Tell her this
And more,—
That the king of the seas
Weeps too, old, helpless man.
The bustling fates
Heap his hands with corpses
Until he stands like a child,
With surplus of toys."

Thomas Moore

The Fire Worshippers

(Excerpt, Stanza 1)

'Tis moonlight over Oman's Sea;—
  Her banks of pearl and palmy isles
Bask in the night-beam beauteously,
  And her blue waters sleep in smiles.
'Tis moonlight in Harmozia's walls,
And through her Emir's porphyry halls,
Where, some hours since, was heard the swell
Of trumpet and the clash of zel,
Bidding the bright-eyed sun farewell;—
The peaceful sun, whom better suits
  The music of the bulbul's nest,
Or the light touch of lovers' lutes,
  To sing him to his golden rest.
All hush'd—there's not a breeze in motion;
The shore is silent as the ocean.
If zephyrs come, so light they come,
  Nor leaf is stirr'd nor wave is driven;—
The wind-tower on the Emir's dome
  Can hardly win a breath from heaven.

Dante Alighieri

The Sailing of Ulysses

Translated by Henry Wadsworth Longfellow

                    When I

From Circe had departed, who concealed me
  More than a year there near unto Gaeta,
  Or ever yet Aeneas named it so,

Nor fondness for my son, nor reverence
  For my old father, nor the due affection
  Which joyous should have made Penelope,

Could overcome within me the desire
  I had to be experienced of the world,
  And of the vice and virtue of mankind;

But I put forth on the high open sea
  With one sole ship, and that small company
  By which I never had deserted been.

Both of the shores I saw as far as Spain,
  Far as Morocco, and the isle of Sardes,
  And the others which that sea bathes round about.

I and my company were old and slow
  When at that narrow passage we arrived
  Where Hercules his landmarks set as signals,

That man no farther onward should adventure.
  On the right hand behind me left I Seville,
  And on the other already had left Ceuta.

"O brothers, who amid a hundred thousand
  Perils," I said, "have come unto the West,
  To this so inconsiderable vigil

Which is remaining of your senses still,
  Be ye unwilling to deny the knowledge,
  Following the sun, of the unpeopled world.

Consider ye the seed from which ye sprang;
  Ye were not made to live like unto brutes,
  But for pursuit of virtue and of knowledge."

So eager did I render my companions,
  With this brief exhortation, for the voyage,
  That then I hardly could have held them back.

And having turned our stern unto the morning,
  We of the oars made wings for our mad flight,
  Evermore gaining on the larboard side.

Already all the stars of the other pole
  The night beheld, and ours so very low
  It did not rise above the ocean floor.

Five times rekindled and as many quenched
  Had been the splendor underneath the moon,
  Since we had entered into the deep pass,

When there appeared to us a mountain, dim
　From distance, and it seemed to me so high
　As I had never any one beheld.

Joyful were we, and soon it turned to weeping;
　For out of the new land a whirlwind rose,
　And smote upon the forepart of the ship.

Three times it made her whirl with all the waters,
　At the fourth time it made the stern uplift,
　And the prow downward go, as pleased Another,

Until the sea above us closed again.

Alfred, Lord Tennyson

On a Desert Island

(Excerpt from *Enoch Arden*)

  The mountain wooded to the peak, the lawns
And winding glades high up like ways to Heaven,
The slender coco's drooping crown of plumes,
The lightning flash of insect and of bird,
The lustre of the long convolvuluses,
That coil'd around the stately stems, and ran
Ev'n to the limit of the land, the glows
And glories of the broad belt of the world,
All these he saw; but what he fain had seen
He could not see, the kindly human face,
Nor ever hear a kindly voice, but heard
The myriad shriek of wheeling ocean-fowl,
The league-long roller thundering on the reef,
The moving whisper of huge trees that branch'd
And blossom'd in the zenith, or the sweep
Of some precipitous rivulet to the wave,
As down the shores he ranged, or all day long
Sat often in the seaward-gazing gorge,
A shipwreck'd sailor, waiting for a sail:
No sail from day to day, but every day
The sunrise broken into scarlet shafts
Among the palms and ferns and precipices;

The blaze upon the waters to the east;
The blaze upon his island overhead;
The blaze upon the waters to the west;
Then the great stars that globed themselves in Heaven,
The hollower-bellowing ocean, and again
The scarlet shafts of sunrise—but no sail.

Henry Wadsworth Longfellow

Seaweed

When descends on the Atlantic
  The gigantic
Storm-wind of the equinox,
Landward in his wrath he scourges
  The toiling surges,
Laden with seaweed from the rocks:

From Bermuda's reefs; from edges
  Of sunken ledges,
In some far-off, bright Azore;
From Bahama, and the dashing,
  Silver-flashing
Surges of San Salvador;

From the tumbling surf, that buries
  The Orkneyan skerries,
Answering the hoarse Hebrides;
And from wrecks of ships, and drifting
  Spars, uplifting
On the desolate, rainy seas;—

Ever drifting, drifting, drifting
  On the shifting
Currents of the restless main;
Till in sheltered coves, and reaches
  Of sandy beaches,
All have found repose again.

So when storms of wild emotion
　Strike the ocean
Of the poet's soul, erelong
From each cave and rocky fastness,
　In its vastness,
Floats some fragment of a song:

From the far-off isles enchanted,
　Heaven has planted
With the golden fruit of Truth;
From the flashing surf, whose vision
　Gleams Elysian
In the tropic clime of Youth;

From the strong Will, and the Endeavor
　That forever
Wrestle with the tides of Fate;
From the wreck of Hopes far-scattered,
　Tempest-shattered,
Floating waste and desolate;—

Ever drifting, drifting, drifting
　On the shifting
Currents of the restless heart;
Till at length in books recorded,
　They, like hoarded
Household words, no more depart.

Thomas Lovell Beddoes

To Sea, to Sea!

To sea, to sea! The calm is o'er;
  The wanton water leaps in sport,
And rattles down the pebbly shore;
  The dolphin wheels, the sea-cows snort,
And unseen Mermaids' pearly song
Comes bubbling up, the weeds among.
  Fling broad the sail, dip deep the oar:
  To sea, to sea! the calm is o'er.

To sea, to sea! our wide-winged bark
  Shall billowy cleave its sunny way,
And with its shadow, fleet and dark,
  Break the caved Tritons' azure day,
Like mighty eagle soaring light
O'er antelopes on Alpine height.
  The anchor heaves, the ship swings free,
  The sails swell full. To sea, to sea!

George Shepard Burleigh

An Ocean Sunrise

Like frosted silver in the earth's broad palm
  The ocean lay, unmoving as the sky,
  When the sky caught, from morning's opening eye,
Ineffable splendors, and from earth the balm
Of all the flowers whose sweetness was a psalm
  Sung out by every bird-throat audibly.
  The soft, warm light reflected from on high
Shed vapory gold on ocean's waveless calm.
Out of the sea the sun rose royally,
  And on the sea its burning image flung,
  And to the sea that burning image clung,
As the orb climbed in double majesty;
A fiery isthmus stretched its arm between
Two continents of fire in passing splendor seen.

Ralph Waldo Emerson

Seashore

I heard or seemed to hear the chiding Sea
Say, Pilgrim, why so late and slow to come?
Am I not always here, thy summer home?
Is not my voice thy music, morn and eve?
My breath thy healthful climate in the heats,
My touch thy antidote, my bay thy bath?
Was ever building like my terraces?
Was ever couch magnificent as mine?
Lie on the warm rock-ledges, and there learn
A little hut suffices like a town.
I make your sculptured architecture vain,
Vain beside mine. I drive my wedges home,
And carve the coastwise mountain into caves.
Lo! here is Rome and Nineveh and Thebes,
Karnak and Pyramid and Giant's Stairs
Half piled or prostrate; and my newest slab
Older than all thy race.

                  Behold the Sea,
The opaline, the plentiful and strong,
Yet beautiful as is the rose in June,
Fresh as the trickling rainbow of July;
Sea full of food, the nourisher of kinds,
Purger of earth, and medicine of men;
Creating a sweet climate by my breath,
Washing out harms and griefs from memory,
And, in my mathematic ebb and flow,
Giving a hint of that which changes not.

Rich are the sea-gods:—who gives gifts but they?
They grope the sea for pearls, but more than pearls:
They pluck Force thence, and give it to the wise.
For every wave is wealth to Daedalus,
Wealth to the cunning artist who can work
This matchless strength. Where shall he find, O waves!
A load your Atlas shoulders cannot lift?

  I with my hammer pounding evermore
The rocky coast, smite Andes into dust,
Strewing my bed, and, in another age,
Rebuild a continent of better men.
Then I unbar the doors: my paths lead out
The exodus of nations: I dispersed
Men to all shores that front the hoary main.

  I too have arts and sorceries;
Illusion dwells forever with the wave.
I know what spells are laid. Leave me to deal
With credulous and imaginative man;
For, though he scoop my water in his palm,
A few rods off he deems it gems and clouds.
Planting strange fruits and sunshine on the shore,
I make some coast alluring, some lone isle,
To distant men, who must go there, or die.

John Boyle O'Reilly

The Flying Dutchman

Long time ago, from Amsterdam
a vessel sailed away,—
As fair a craft as ever flung
aside the laughing spray.
Upon the shore were tearful eyes,
and scarfs were in the air,
As to her, o'er the Zuyder Zee,
went fond adieu and prayer;
And brave hearts, yearning shoreward
from the outward-going ship,
Felt lingering kisses clinging still
to tear-wet cheek and lip.
She steered for some far eastern clime,
and, as she skimmed the seas,
Each taper mast was bending
like a rod before the breeze.

Her captain was a stalwart man,—
an iron heart had he.—
From childhood's days he sailed
upon the rolling Zuyder Zee:
He nothing feared upon the earth,
and scarcely heaven feared,
He would have dared and done
whatever mortal man had dared!
He looked aloft, where high in air
the pennant cut the blue,
And every rope and spar and sail

was firm and strong and true.
He turned him from the swelling sail
to gaze upon the shore,—
Ah! little thought the skipper then
'twould meet his eye no more;
He dreamt not that an awful doom
was hanging o'er his ship,
That Vanderdecken's name would yet
make pale the speaker's lip.
The vessel bounded on her way,
and spire and dome went down,—
Ere darkness fell, beneath the wave
had sunk the distant town.
No more, no more, ye hapless crew,
shall Holland meet your eye.
In lingering hope and keen suspense,
maid, wife, and child shall die!

Away, away the vessel speeds,
till sea and sky alone
Are round her, as her coarse she steers
across the torrid zone.
Away, until the North Star fades,
the Southern Cross is high,
And myriad gems of brightest beam
are sparkling in the sky.
The tropic winds are left behind;
she nears the Cape of Storms,
Where awful Tempest ever sits
enthroned in wild alarms;
Where Ocean in his anger shakes
aloft his foamy crest,

Disdainful of the weakly toys
that ride upon his breast.
Fierce swell the winds and waters
round the Dutchman's gallant ship,
But, to their rage, defiance rings
from Vanderdecken's lip:
Impotent they to make him swerve,
their might he dares despise,
And straight he holds his onward course,
and wind and wave defies.
For days and nights he struggles
in the weird, unearthly fight.
His brow is bent, his eye is fierce,
but looks of deep affright
Amongst the mariners go round,
as hopelessly they steer:
They do not dare to murmur,
but they whisper what they fear.
Their black-browed captain awes them:
'neath his darkened eye they quail,
And in a grim and sullen mood
their bitter fate bewail.
As some fierce rider ruthless spurs
a timid, wavering horse,
He drives his shapely vessel,
and they watch the reckless course,
Till once again their skipper's laugh
is flung upon the blast;
The placid ocean smiles beyond,
the dreaded Cape is passed!

Away across the Indian main
the vessel northward glides;
A thousand murmuring ripples break
along her graceful sides:
The perfumed breezes fill her sails,—
her destined port she nears,—
The captain's brow has lost its frown,
the mariners their fears.
"Land ho!" at length the welcome sound
the watchful sailor sings,
And soon within an Indian bay
the ship at anchor swings.
Not idle then the busy crew:
ere long the spacious hold
Is emptied of its western freight,
and stored with silk and gold.

Again the ponderous anchor's weighed;
the shore is left behind,
The snowy sails are bosomed out
before the favoring wind.
Across the warm blue Indian sea
the vessel southward flies,
And once again the North Star fades
and Austral beacons rise.
For home she steers! she seems to know
and answer to the word,
And swifter skims the burnished deep,
like some fair ocean bird.
"For home! for home!" the merry crew
with gladsome voices cry,

And dark-browed Vanderdecken
has a mild light in his eye.

But once again the Cape draws near,
and furious billows rise;
And still the daring Dutchman's laugh
the hurricane defies.
But wildly shrieked the tempest
ere the scornful sound had died,
A warning to the daring man
to curb his impious pride.
A crested mountain struck the ship,
and like a frighted bird
She trembled 'neath the awful shock.
Then Vanderdecken heard
A pleading voice within the gale,—
his better angel spoke,
But fled before his scowling look,
as mast-high mountains broke
Around the trembling vessel,
till the crew with terror paled;
But Vanderdecken never flinched,
nor 'neath the thunders quailed.
With folded arms and stern-pressed lips,
dark anger in his eye,
He answered back the threatening frown
that lowered o'er the sky.
With fierce defiance in his heart,
and scornful look of flame,
He spoke, and thus with impious voice
blasphemed God's holy name:—

"Howl on, ye winds! ye tempests, howl!
your rage is spent in vain:
Despite your strength, your frowns, your hate,
I'll ride upon the main.
Defiance to your idle shrieks!
I'll sail upon my path:
I cringe not for thy Maker's smile,—
I care not for His wrath!"

He ceased. An awful silence fell:
the tempest and the sea
Were hushed in sudden stillness
by the Ruler's dread decree.
The ship was riding motionless
within the gathering gloom;
The Dutchman stood upon the poop
and heard his dreadful doom.
The hapless crew were on the deck
in swooning terror prone,—
They, too, were bound in fearful fate.
In angered thunder-tone
The judgment words swept o'er the sea:
"Go, wretch, accurst, condemned!
Go sail for ever on the deep,
by shrieking tempests hemmed.
No home, no port, no calm, no rest,
no gentle fav'ring breeze,
Shall ever greet thee. Go, accurst!
and battle with the seas!
Go, braggart! struggle with the storm,
nor ever cease to live,
But bear a million times the pangs

that death and fear can give.
Away! and hide thy guilty head,
a curse to all thy kind
Who ever see thee struggling, wretch,
with ocean and with wind.
Away, presumptuous worm of earth!
Go teach thy fellow-worms
The awful fate that waits on him
who braves the King of Storms!"

'Twas o'er. A lurid lightning flash
lit up the sea and sky
Around and o'er the fated ship;
then rose a wailing cry
From every heart within her,
of keen anguish and despair;
But mercy was for them no more,—
it died away in air.

Once more the lurid light gleamed out,—
the ship was still at rest,
The crew were standing at their posts;
with arms across his breast
Still stood the captain on the poop,
but bent and crouching now
He bowed beneath that fiat dread,
and o'er his swarthy brow
Swept lines of anguish,
as if he a thousand years of pain
Had lived and suffered.
Then across the heaving, angry main
The tempest shrieked triumphant,

and the angry waters hissed
Their vengeful hate against the toy
they oftentimes had kissed.
And ever through the midnight storm
that hapless crew must speed;
They try to round the stormy Cape,
but never can succeed.
And oft when gales are wildest,
and the lightning's vivid sheen
Flashes back the ocean's anger,
still the Phantom Ship is seen
Ever sailing to the southward
in the fierce tornado's swoop,
With her ghostly crew and canvas,
and her captain on the poop,
Unrelenting, unforgiven;
and 'tis said that every word
Of his blasphemous defiance
still upon the gale is heard!
But Heaven help the ship
near which the dismal sailor steers,—
The doom of those is sealed
to whom that Phantom Ship appears:
They'll never reach their destined port,—
they'll see their homes no more,—
They who see the Flying Dutchman—
never, never reach the shore!

Charlotte Perkins Gilman

The Rock and the Sea

The Rock

I am the Rock, presumptuous Sea!
I am set to encounter thee.
Angry and loud or gentle and still,
I am set here to limit thy power, and I will!
      I am the Rock!

I am the Rock. From age to age
I scorn thy fury and dare thy rage.
Scarred by frost and worn by time,
Brown with weed and green with slime,
Thou may'st drench and defile me and spit in my face,
But while I am here thou keep'st thy place!
      I am the Rock!

I am the Rock, beguiling Sea!
I know thou art fair as fair can be,
With golden glitter and silver sheen,
And bosom of blue and garments of green.
Thou may'st pat my cheek with baby hands,
And lap my feet in diamond sands,
And play before me as children play;
But plead as thou wilt, I bar the way!
      I am the Rock!

I am the Rock. Black midnight falls;
The terrible breakers rise like walls;
With curling lips and gleaming teeth

They plunge and tear at my bones beneath.
Year upon year they grind and beat
In storms of thunder and storms of sleet,—
Grind and beat and wrestle and tear,
But the rock they beat on is always there!
      I am the Rock!

The Sea

I am the Sea. I hold the land
As one holds an apple in his hand.
Hold it fast with sleepless eyes,
Watching the continents sink and rise.
Out of my bosom the mountains grow,
Back to its depths they crumble slow;
The earth is a helpless child to me.
      I am the Sea!

I am the Sea. When I draw back
Blossom and verdure follow my track,
And the land I leave grows proud and fair,
For the wonderful race of man is there;
And the winds of heaven wail and cry
While the nations rise and reign and die,
Living and dying in folly and pain,
While the laws of the universe thunder in vain.
What is the folly of man to me?
      I am the Sea!

I am the Sea. The earth I sway;
Granite to me is potter's clay;
Under the touch of my careless waves
It rises in turrets and sinks in caves;

The iron cliffs that edge the land
I grind to pebbles and sift to sand,
And beach-grass bloweth and children play
In what were the rocks of yesterday.
It is but a moment of sport to me.
          I am the Sea!

I am the Sea. In my bosom deep
Wealth and Wonder and Beauty sleep;
Wealth and Wonder and Beauty rise
In changing splendor of sunset skies,
And comfort the earth with rains and snows
Till waves the harvest and laughs the rose.
Flower and forest and child of breath
With me have life—without me, death.
What if the ships go down in me?
          I am the Sea!

Emily Dickinson

I Think that the Root of the Wind Is Water—

I think that the Root of the Wind is Water—
It would not sound so deep
Were it a Firmamental Product—
Airs no Oceans keep—
Mediterranean intonations—
To a Current's ear—
There is a maritime conviction
In the Atmosphere.

Rainer Maria Rilke

Song of the Sea

Translated by Gene Hult

(Capri, Piccola Marina)

Immemorial zephyr,
sea-wind of night:
  you come not for anyone;
if one watches,
he must see how he
weathers you:
  immemorial zephyr,
which gusts
unto primordial stone,
you are purest space
rending from a distance. . . .

Oh, how do you feel
raising a fig tree
up in the moonlight?

Nathaniel Hawthorne

The Ocean

The Ocean has its silent caves,
Deep, quiet, and alone;
Though there be fury on the waves,
Beneath them there is none.
The awful spirits of the deep
Hold their communion there;
And there are those for whom we weep,
The young, the bright, the fair.

Calmly the wearied seamen rest
Beneath their own blue sea.
The ocean solitudes are blest,
For there is purity.
The earth has guilt, the earth has care,
Unquiet are its graves;
But peaceful sleep is ever there,
Beneath the dark blue waves.

Sara Teasdale

Sea Longing

A thousand miles beyond this sun-steeped wall
Somewhere the waves creep cool along the sand,
The ebbing tide forsakes the listless land
With the old murmur, long and musical;
The windy waves mount up and curve and fall,
And round the rocks the foam blows up like snow,—
Tho' I am inland far, I hear and know,
For I was born the sea's eternal thrall.
I would that I were there and over me
The cold insistence of the tide would roll,
Quenching this burning thing men call the soul,—
Then with the ebbing I should drift and be
Less than the smallest shell along the shoal,
Less than the sea-gulls calling to the sea.

Lord Byron

The Ocean

(Excerpt from *Childe Harold's Pilgrimage*)

CLXXIX.
Roll on, thou deep and dark blue Ocean—roll!
Ten thousand fleets sweep over thee in vain;
Man marks the earth with ruin—his control
Stops with the shore;—upon the watery plain
The wrecks are all thy deed, nor doth remain
A shadow of man's ravage, save his own,
When, for a moment, like a drop of rain,
He sinks into thy depths with bubbling groan,
Without a grave, unknell'd, uncoffin'd, and unknown.

CLXXX.
His steps are not upon thy paths;—thy fields
Are not a spoil for him,—thou dost arise
And shake him from thee; the vile strength he wields
For earth's destruction thou dost all despise,
Spurning him from thy bosom to the skies,
And send'st him, shivering in thy playful spray
And howling, to his gods, where haply lies
His petty hope in some near port or bay,
And dashest him again to earth:—there let him lay.

CLXXXI.
The armaments which thunderstrike the walls
Of rock-built cities, bidding nations quake,
And monarchs tremble in their capitals,
The oak leviathans, whose huge ribs make

Their clay creator the vain title take
Of lord of thee, and arbiter of war;
These are thy toys, and, as the snowy flake,
They melt into thy yeast of waves, which mar
Alike the Armada's pride, or spoils of Trafalgar.

CLXXXII.
Thy shores are empires, changed in all save thee—
Assyria, Greece, Rome, Carthage, what are they?
Thy waters washed them power while they were free,
And many a tyrant since: their shores obey
The stranger, slave, or savage; their decay
Has dried up realms to deserts: not so thou,
Unchangeable save to thy wild waves' play—
Time writes no wrinkle on thine azure brow—
Such as creation's dawn beheld, thou rollest now.

CLXXXIII.
Thou glorious mirror, where the Almighty's form
Glasses itself in tempests; in all time,
Calm or convulsed—in breeze, or gale, or storm,
Icing the pole, or in the torrid clime
Dark-heaving;—boundless, endless, and sublime—
The image of Eternity—the throne
Of the Invisible; even from out thy slime
The monsters of the deep are made; each zone
Obeys thee; thou goest forth, dread, fathomless, alone.

CLXXXIV.
And I have loved thee, Ocean! and my joy
Of youthful sports was on thy breast to be
Borne, like thy bubbles, onward: from a boy

I wanton'd with thy breakers—they to me
Were a delight; and if the freshening sea
Made them a terror—'twas a pleasing fear,
For I was as it were a child of thee,
And trusted to thy billows far and near,
And laid my hand upon thy mane—as I do here.

Dante Gabriel Rossetti

The Sea-Limits

Consider the sea's listless chime:
  Time's self it is, made audible,—
  The murmur of the earth's own shell.
Secret continuance sublime
  Is the sea's end: our sight may pass
  No furlong further. Since time was,
This sound hath told the lapse of time.

No quiet, which is death's,—it hath
  The mournfulness of ancient life,
  Enduring always at dull strife.
As the world's heart of rest and wrath,
  Its painful pulse is in the sands.
  Last utterly, the whole sky stands,
Grey and not known, along its path.

Listen alone beside the sea,
  Listen alone among the woods;
  Those voices of twin solitudes
Shall have one sound alike to thee:
  Hark where the murmurs of thronged men
  Surge and sink back and surge again,—
Still the one voice of wave and tree.

Gather a shell from the strown beach
  And listen at its lips: they sigh
  The same desire and mystery,
The echo of the whole sea's speech.

And all mankind is thus at heart
  Not anything but what thou art:
And Earth, Sea, Man, are all in each.

D. H. Lawrence

The Mystic Blue

Out of the darkness, fretted sometimes in its sleeping,
Jets of sparks in fountains of blue come leaping
To sight, revealing a secret, numberless secrets keeping.

Sometimes the darkness trapped within a wheel
Runs into speed like a dream, the blue of the steel
Showing the rocking darkness now a-reel.

And out of the invisible, streams of bright blue drops
Rain from the showery heavens, and bright blue crops
Surge from the under-dark to their ladder-tops.

And all the manifold blue and joyous eyes,
The rainbow arching over in the skies,
New sparks of wonder opening in surprise.

All these pure things come foam and spray of the sea
Of Darkness abundant, which shaken mysteriously,
Breaks into dazzle of living, as dolphins that leap from the sea
Of midnight shake it to fire, so the secret of death we see.

Arthur Guiterman

A Sea Dream

Off the coast of the Isle of Peril,
  In the depths of the heaving tides,
All aglow through its walls of beryl
  Is the house where the Sea King bides.

There he laughs when the norther rages,
  There he dreams while the surges drone;
And the spoils of the fleets of ages
  Are the tithes of his sapphire throne.

Through the spray of the booming waters,
  Through the chant of the swinging sea,
Thrills the song of the Sea King's daughters—
  And it comes as a call to me.

Oh, the sky is a turquoise chalice
  And the bar is a golden glaive,
As I plunge to the Sea King's palace
  In the gulfs of the cool, green wave!

Emily Dickinson

Exultation Is the Going

Exultation is the going
Of an inland soul to sea—
Past the Houses,
past the Headlands,
Into deep Eternity—

Bred as we, among the mountains,
Can the sailor understand
The divine intoxication
Of the first league out from Land?

Thomas S. Jones, Jr.

Dusk at Sea

To-night eternity alone is near:
The sea, the sunset, and the darkening blue;
Within their shelter is no space for fear,
Only the wonder that such things are true.

The thought of you is like the dusk at sea—
Space and wide freedom and old shores left far,
The shelter of a lone immensity
Sealed by the sunset and the evening star.

John Sterling

The Two Oceans

Two seas amid the night,
  In the moonshine roll and sparkle,
Now spread in the silver light,
  Now sadden, and wail, and darkle.
The one has a billowy motion,
  And from land to land it gleams;
The other is sleep's wide ocean,
  And its glimmering waves are dreams.
The one with murmur and roar
  Bears fleets around coast and islet;
The other, without a shore,
  Ne'er knew the track of a pilot.

Bliss Carman

A Son of the Sea

I was born for deep-sea faring;
I was bred to put to sea;
Stories of my father's daring
Filled me at my mother's knee.

I was sired among the surges;
I was cubbed beside the foam;
All my heart is in its verges,
And the sea wind is my home.

All my boyhood, from far vernal
Bourns of being, came to me
Dream-like, plangent, and eternal
Memories of the plunging sea.

Robert Louis Stevenson

A Visit from the Sea

Far from the loud sea beaches
  Where he goes fishing and crying,
Here in the inland garden
  Why is the sea-gull flying?

Here are no fish to dive for;
  Here is the corn and lea;
Here are the green trees rustling.
  Hie away home to sea!

Fresh is the river water
  And quiet among the rushes;
This is no home for the sea-gull
  But for the rooks and thrushes.

Pity the bird that has wandered!
  Pity the sailor ashore!
Hurry him home to the ocean,
  Let him come here no more!

High on the sea-cliff ledges
  The white gulls are trooping and crying,
Here among rooks and roses,
  Why is the sea-gull flying?

Elizabeth Barrett Browning

The Sea-Mew

> Affectionately Inscribed to M. E. H.

I.
How joyously the young sea-mew
Lay dreaming on the waters blue,
Whereon our little bark had thrown
A little shade, the only one,—
But shadows ever man pursue.

II.
Familiar with the waves and free
As if their own white foam were he,
His heart upon the heart of ocean
Lay learning all its mystic motion,
And throbbing to the throbbing sea.

III.
And such a brightness in his eye,
As if the ocean and the sky
Within him had lit up and nurst
A soul God gave him not at first,
To comprehend their majesty.

IV.
We were not cruel, yet did sunder
His white wing from the blue waves under,
And bound it, while his fearless eyes
Shone up to ours in calm surprise,
As deeming us some ocean wonder!

V.
We bore our ocean bird unto
A grassy place, where he might view
The flowers that curtsy to the bees,
The waving of the tall green trees,
The falling of the silver dew.

VI.
But flowers of earth were pale to him
Who had seen the rainbow fishes swim;
And when earth's dew around him lay
He thought of ocean's wingèd spray,
And his eye waxèd sad and dim.

VII.
The green trees round him only made
A prison with their darksome shade;
And drooped his wing, and mournèd he
For his own boundless glittering sea—
Albeit he knew not they could fade.

VIII.
Then One her gladsome face did bring,
Her gentle voice's murmuring,
In ocean's stead his heart to move
And teach him what was human love—
He thought it a strange, mournful thing.

VIX.
He lay down in his grief to die,
(First looking to the sea-like sky
That hath no waves!), because, alas!
Our human touch did on him pass,
And with our touch, our agony.

Eva L. Ogden

The Sea

She was rich and of high degree;
A poor and unknown artist he.
"Paint me," she said, "a view of the sea."

So he painted the sea as it looked the day
That Aphrodite arose from its spray;
And it broke, as she gazed on its face the while,
Into its countless-dimpled smile.
"What a poky, stupid picture!" said she.
"I don't believe he *can* paint the sea!"

Then he painted a raging, tossing sea,
Storming, with fierce and sudden shock,
wild cries, and writhing tongues of foam,
A towering, mighty fastness-rock.
In its sides, above those leaping crests,
The thronging sea-birds built their nests.
"What a disagreeable daub!" said she.
"Why, it isn't anything like the sea!"

Then he painted a stretch of hot, brown sand,
With a big hotel on either hand,
And a handsome pavilion for the band—
Not a sign of the water to be seen
Except one faint little streak of green.
"What a perfectly exquisite picture!" said she.
"It's the very *image* of the sea!"

Edna St. Vincent Millay

Exiled

Searching my heart for its true sorrow,
　This is the thing I find to be:
That I am weary of words and people,
　Sick of the city, wanting the sea;

Wanting the sticky, salty sweetness
　Of the strong wind and shattered spray;
Wanting the loud sound and the soft sound
　Of the big surf that breaks all day.

Always before about my dooryard,
　Marking the reach of the winter sea,
Rooted in sand and dragging drift-wood,
　Straggled the purple wild sweet-pea;

Always I climbed the wave at morning,
　Shook the sand from my shoes at night,
That now am caught beneath great buildings,
　Stricken with noise, confused with light.

If I could hear the green piles groaning
　Under the windy wooden piers,
See once again the bobbing barrels,
　And the black sticks that fence the weirs,

If I could see the weedy mussels
　Crusting the wrecked and rotting hulls,
Hear once again the hungry crying
　Overhead, of the wheeling gulls,

Feel once again the shanty straining
  Under the turning of the tide,
Fear once again the rising freshet,
  Dread the bell in the fog outside,—

I should be happy,—that was happy
  All day long on the coast of Maine!
I have a need to hold and handle
  Shells and anchors and ships again!

I should be happy, that am happy
  Never at all since I came here.
I am too long away from water.
  I have a need of water near.

William Wordsworth

The Sea Shell

(Excerpt from *The Excursion*)

       I have seen
A curious child, who dwelt upon a tract
Of inland ground, applying to his ear
The convolutions of a smooth-lipped shell;
To which, in silence hushed, his very soul
Listened intensely; and his countenance soon
Brightened with joy; for murmurings from within
Were heard, sonorous cadences! whereby,
To his belief, the monitor expressed
Mysterious union with its native sea.
Even such a shell the universe itself
Is to the ear of Faith; and there are times,
I doubt not, when to you it doth impart
Authentic tidings of invisible things;
Of ebb and flow, and ever-during power;
And central peace, subsisting at the heart
Of endless agitation.

Current

Jenny Blackford

The Way the Water

The way the water washes
and sweeps foaming over deep-cracked
wet brown rocks,

swirls in the crevices the swishy
salty leaves greener than lettuce,
softer than silk jelly,

the stomach-footed shelly beasts
their tender bellies
sucking hard the rock,

the worm-flowers of anemones
feeling for tiny fish
with long bright poisoned fingers,

the five-pointed shining things
fallen from the sky above
into the blue below,

and the ten-legged sideways
scuttlers, so succulent
in their thin armor,

each of them living
its own wet
wave-washed life.

The way the foaming white
sloshes back to sea messy
as bubbles in a giant's sink

then breaks itself, smooth
green patches spreading
pale with still-dissolved sky.

The way the green defeats
the foam each and every time
until the next white wave.

Ben Bever

Sea-glass

The green winter Mediterranean
rattles like grizzled, tubercular lungs,
a million fingers wearing away
moments like the fallen pillars of
Appolonia, strewn up the beach.

If you know how and where to look,
specks of Roman glass cower beneath them,
ghost crabs in their tunnels, out of reach.
It comes in pale, translucent blues, always
smooth and round from a millennium of slow,
wet thievery—salt and sand leaching thin
bottle flesh, leaving only round pebbles
of color for visiting tourists.

David Holper

To Pewetole Island

I.
I walk into pale winter sunshine
trudging northwards along the shore. Just below me
high tide stretches, hissing—and just beyond
the waveline, the stacks tower starkly.
Staring at this landscape, I recognize
what one can know with certainty:
birth, age, the slow surety
of our race preparing to pass. What does it matter,
I wonder, in the presence of such austere forms:
hardened sentinels of melange;
the softer sedimentary deposits
long waved away. After my race
vanishes, Sitka spruce and juniper will still bend
against the wind. Their trunks will trace the outline
of chert, sandstone, greenstone, basalt.

II.
Where the beach narrows, I step into the blind
erasure of fog. So defined in sunshine,
the sea and stacks seem befuddled in this halfworld
of sun and mist. The waves menace,
the tide still rising. Certainty fades,
and I am left in a blurred gray microcosm
of sand beneath my feet; macrocosm,
the impossibility to repair all we have damaged.
How should I understand this, our careless need?
I wonder if in the minutes after I have passed

will the surf will slam shut the door of my retreat.
I scramble ahead of the waves,
walking directly into shadow.

III.
No one follows. My footsteps
erased even before I am out of sight. The fog
thickens: the stacks, the kelp, the cobble fade.
I sense more than see Pewetole Island looming ahead.
Less than a month ago, someone torched
the Sitka Spruce. For what reason, I wonder,
but I doubt I—or anyone—will ever know.
For three days it burned. Where I stop
the beach surrenders to the sea. The waves circle
the island from both directions, confused
as they touch; I can only smell
the burned timber ahead.
Here I come to see
all that is invisible: the source
of life, what stands athwart the other side.
In this moment, I know with certainty
what is just ahead. How, you ask?
I stood at the dark edge, sensing all
still unseen.

Carol Alena Aronoff

The Muse

has fastened her teeth to my leg
and hidden me from the moon. Her outer
shell—coarse, brown, ridged. Her other
side—smooth, blue pearl, lights me
in tiny sparks when I face away from sun.

Delicate as fern-like sea hair, unbending
as dead man's fingers, she has torn my heart
from its common moorings and insisted
I listen to the ocean. Really listen.
More than to tide and wave, to curl and froth.

Even gull songs are beside the point.
It takes slowing time, this kind of listening.
Deep in the marrow of place, the belly
of silence. Where I can feel seeds
germinate before there are names.

I am patient as a turtle sunning on lava.
For now, I relinquish the need to know.
Canaries chatter without my attending, fish
jump in tide pools, splashing unnoticed.
Exhilarated, I write to the incoming tide.

Joel Allegretti

The Sea at Our Door

For my mother, 1929-2005

a butterfly batted its flame-and-leopard wings
against the salt breeze, flickered
through the sea grass maze like a dyed paper
likeness of itself and witnessed this:

a dolphin at the end of her day languished ashore;
her flipper spaded the beach; her tail begged the foam;
mourned by starfish, who envied their namesakes
buttoned in the warm spread of sky—
(we all want the property of light)—she nuzzled
the sand while her child bleated from the shallows;

the elegy wind sang down her back and bowed
her dorsal fin like a viola; a halo of gulls wheeled
overhead; she drank in their bony cackles
as she surrendered to a part of the earth
she was never meant to know;

night keeps its promise;
it comes to each of us; somewhere in the ocean's
twilight shushing was the memory, now as lost
as a drowned ship, of joyful pirouettes
against a gracious moon;

the butterfly alighted on the pedestal of her snout,
its stuttering wings rousing her grateful anticipation
that the blue sweep above was another sea;
close your eyes, the butterfly said, it's good to close them.

Janet Barry

wrack line

I dance the edges of my dream,
a thin tide swelling across smooth sand,
a wrack line of twisted kelp, memories,
detritus of a day, a week, an offshore wreck
washed plank by plank to my feet.

there—a jumble of snails, mussels,
a dented cooking pan, dead gull,
a copy of my birth certificate.
an old sweater fading gray
among the sodden fishing line.

there—a face, tangled hair,
is it mine? a cigarette lighter,
a collection of whiskey bottles,
a black feather caught in the scree,
waving steadily to each passing breeze.

a flip-flop, a bikini top,
a broken mermaid's purse,
tiny skates escaped to the open sea,
the birth pouch left to crawl
among delicate broken bones,

my left hand, a pelvis, a tooth
bleached baby white, and there—
a smooth pebble of quartz, small

sun as I dart through this dark dream,
clutch it from the sea-tangle,
fling it back to the waves.

Elizabeth Ruth Deyro

Let the Oceans Speak for Me

Cold waters caress my feet like lovers kept apart
by chance. Foam meets flesh, flesh kisses sand
like wet clay against my soles—I press harder,
frail attempt to leave imprints of a soul wandering
the oceans on barefoot. I watch the waves tuck
the earth back into its initial form, taking my mark
with the constant cleansing.

I descend further
with every step toward the horizon.
Let the ocean paint me blue, take
my half-full vessel and lead me to depths
unbeknown to man. I shall hold my breath
until the air kisses me back to life.

Gene Hult

Sea Stack

I hope you'll meet me
in a moment of saline lucidity.

When I'm not depressed
by the distressed furniture
hulking on these sandy floorboards
like flotsam tumbled and spat ashore
from history's turbulence.

Ice-spun fog flows and ebbs
like nutrient-rich tides,
lapping at my sudden translucency.

It may mean a fight
if I'm to admit
that your insoluble boulder
describes the surge of my current.

Equipped with parasitic seed pods,
I strew my children of espionage
into the wet wind.
They report to me
with deep sea sonar
and a huge margin of error.

I peer into what happens next,
a sailor's prayer for a red moon tonight,
and wonder how many regrets

about the unfinished are required
for advanced placement in the afterlife.

I agree it's unfair to pose scenarios
with preprojected outcomes—
skewing toward a rocky outcropping
of self-fulfilling prophecy,
no matter how grotesque
the shaping desires of my ocean.

I want to camouflage
the sinkhole entrance
to this surging wound
with bleached tree branches
and detached fronds of seaweed
in the hope you'll fall in.

Paul Magrs

Across the Ocean

I thought I'd never seen the ocean
Everything was shallow
The mackerel grey
The slubbed silk
The drag queen silver
Eye shadow
Of the North Sea
And the faded denim crotch of the Med

I'd been nowhere profound
Plumbed no great depths
Never swam with strange beasties
With luminous fangs
Never sank to any great depravity

Or inched along through wreckage
And hulks, feeling in the dark
For skeletons of men with violins
Or caskets of jewels
And the stories of all those relations
From Ireland and Tyneside
Who sailed
So long ago
Vanishing into America

But of course
I've seen oceans:
Peering down from

Tiny windows
Avid
And appalled

I've stared down
Into the
Abyss
With a gin
And tonic
I've considered
The sublime
With a rug
On my lap
Blinking tired eyes

And
Marveling
For a hundred years.

Lynne Viti

Lament

I dreamed my father was the ocean—
salt water lapping, reclaiming the beaches—
or he was Poseidon, with his trident, ruling the seas.
Only my father didn't rule the water.

The salt waters of the bay and the booze
conspired to push the boat on which he dozed,
sunburned, sated with whisky. He was slammed
against the pilings of a small bridge. He never
walked right again. His football days were long
over. Now he couldn't even show me
how to run for yardage after catching the pass.

He couldn't drive a standard because his ankle
screamed when he depressed the clutch.
From then on it was automatic Chevys for him,
all the way, power steering, too. He graduated
from crutches to brace and cane, one from Mexico,
a green snake curling up the cane,
swallowing the tail of a black snake.

There were no ramps in those days, no special
parking places, no seats in the aisle, no elevators at
the stadium. He held up his cane, in the car window,
called Hey, Mac! Can I get a good spot up front?

When I walk along the beach, tide on its way in,
winds propelling the water under my feet,

waves so high no one dares wade in,
I know my father was never the sea,
was never king of the sea,
but a toy of the churning gray water.

Suzanne S. Rancourt

The Shores of Methana

The pine here smells like sweet grass.
How curious the waves are
with my squatting on the wet pumice
among human refuse and profound beauty
of natural decay

The bleached Cuttlebones accentuate
the porous reds and blacks of tumbled stones,
their bird breast shapes—
a shield we place in Budgie cages
for their ritual sharpening of beaks

This Poseidic wave a salted poultice
draws love from my chest
the white caps—and smear of salve
as simple as bread to butter
with fruit of jams

These waves barrel roll
like logs of children down summer sloped lawns
or the roll of thumbs across knotted muscles of trauma
that ease out a sigh from lips just barely breaking silence

A mist of skimming gulls and crows
through the cervical straits of volcanic thighs
releases a love that belongs to no human
belongs to the deity of beyond

It is what draws us as a titration
through open mouths of discovery
and bardic tales—no one would know
if you told the truth or lied

This song is a gale of grief and forgiveness
that flip turns after slamming the shores of your heart
This song
is pulled into a desirous love that no man no longer owns
this is the Siren's song and it isn't one of longing
but the songs of the dead for the dead know
that maybe, they made mistakes

Lucinda Marshall

Ebb Tide

At the edge of
our long ago realm,
where sand dollars
were the currency
of childhood kingdoms
built by the sea,

my footing shifts on
permeable shore
as the tide that once
plundered our fortunes
in nightly battle
washes over my toes,

and I wonder
with a fierceness
what becomes of us,
of who we are
in this moment
before the surf falls back.

Alec Solomita

Familiar

I could swear I remember this bird,
one-legged on the watery sand.
Maybe because it looks like
he remembers me. I step
toward him, and instead of the usual
baggy-pants saunter out of range,
he stays put and regards me with
a kind of pity. Eyes crossed, chest out,
the yellow-beaked flyboy looks like he's
thinking of old song titles, "Alone Again,
Naturally." I want to rush him like a kid,
want all of a sudden to kick him into a feathery piñata.
But there's all those guys on the stacked summer porches
drinking Molson Dry and Labatt Blue tallboys
as they watch their girlfriends brush grains of sand
off their burnt bellies.

Joel Allegretti

Gabriel the Beachcomber

The slopping of the sea grew still one night...
                                        Wallace Stevens

The sea brought to mind a glass harmonica,
And all was pianissimo with the world.
There were murmurs in the sand dunes,
Secrets only a tern would know.
A fiddler crab has its own repertory of dances.
The day arrived in a density of splendors.

The sea brought to mind a confectioner's shop,
And all was bittersweet with the world.
There were rumors of a wedding,
A consecration by the jetty stones.
We wondered how roses would fare in the salt air.
The day rejoiced in a density of splendors.

The sea brought to mind a four o'clock tea,
And all was demure with the world.
There was a polyphony of salutations.
The clouds were a flock of parasols.
The gulls were clad in corporate white and grey.
The day wearied of its density of splendors.

The sea brought to mind a family estate,
And all was venerable with the world.
There were recollections in the spindrift,
Testaments embroidered in the coral.

A lighthouse, too, has an autobiography.
The day reminisced in a density of splendors.

The sea brought to mind a greater sea,
And all was marvelous with the world.
There were conjurations in the tide pool,
Traces of the moon at her inventive best.
We saw the shadow of Portugal on the horizon.
The day bid goodnight to its density of splendors.

R. T. Castleberry

The Mission of Water

Waves cluster at the shore.
There is no music to it.
Only smells of brackish marsh, settling musk,
only the debts of sea birds.
Tension tethers the day.
Sunshine isolates each
building, bus, stroller's block,
like letters stroked through a stencil.
I lease my temper to a hoaxing smile,
the vagabond's chronic, covering laugh.
I take a blank wall edge to edge, stripe it
with grievance ink, charcoaled ideograms
of a fisherman collapsed upon his nets,
the shattered hull of an overloaded boat.
I walk closer to the water line,
to the limits of my disfavored name,
that derelict paternity.
Harbor pearls curl at my feet,
color a spoiled blue, boiling under flames.

Bill Cushing

Sailing

>for Joseph Conrad

I have always taken
the four a.m. watch:
those three hours before dawn when,
inhaling the moist sweetness
of a new day, we awake
and escape last night's darkness,
leaving technology
to experience
quiet and primitive satisfaction.
The ocean rushing underneath,
its volume
dependent upon current hull speed,
spills a phosphorescent wake—
the only natural source of light
besides the moon.
Rolling up and down,
swaying into balance
on the balls of my feet while
cradling the warmth
of a mug's contents.
Soon
an orange sliver appears
and grows, as the sun
finds the seam in the weld
that fixes sea to sky.

Ciarán Parkes

Kelp

In his last email he describes kelp
growing taller than the tallest tree
and how Shackleton and his small crew,
seeking help from Elephant Island, knew

they could cling to it as a last resort
if they didn't make landfall before darkness
fell again and how the danger
wasn't so much sinking as colliding

with the jagged coast, the cliffs, like them
all floating up above the highest branches
of kelp they could have twisted into rope
to anchor them, something like the rafts

Aran Islanders made from strands of seaweed
to drift back inland with the tide. He tells
how they made it safe ashore at last, the hull
of the *James Caird* battered, worn thin

as an upturned mussel shell, or maybe
leaves them there, still hanging on somehow
above the kelp, suspended in mid-air.

Lauren Davis

Land Not Required

Make a sailor out of me.
I have been landlocked for so long
on my little black beach,
braiding kelp, christening seagulls.
Your sloop stretches out of the gloom,
sighting my shore. Anchored, salt
in the crease of your wrists. My body
unaccustomed to the sway of water,
first rock me back and forth on sand.
Train me how to hike the mast.
In the berth, let me map oceans
on your chest. I will follow you
anywhere. We will test the theory
of the flat earth, in the morning waking
to a hull of muddled latitudes.
The helm each night unattended.

Agnieszka Filipek

Mermaid

lonely night
surges to my lips
and hangs the moon
around my neck

wrapped in sea foam
I spit stars

my heart
produces pearls
salt crystals
fall from my eyes

and seaweed
pulls me down
into a cold sleep
on the ocean bed

Larry D. Thacker

Fisherman's Runes

A fisherman's certain expected boredom
between stringing bait and the wait,

a time commonly filled with the working
of tools, the nervous cleaning knife,

nicely sharpened that early morning
between long satisfying sips of coffee,

thinking on the day before the day
commences, what it requires in trade,

the fine blade dragged smoothly
over the leaning plank, measured glance

hardly removed from the pole's tip,
testing the flesh of long salted wood

with the blade's eager edge, the pulp,
grayed and greened, softened by the breath

of the sea's constant awareness, deepening
marks worked alongside the others

like a meditation of runic prayers.

Sidney Bending

Dead Zones, Dying Zones

sea lion, harbour seal, sandpiper, scallop

Off the coast of high and higher cities,
whatever we pass through our bodies,
through our sewers to the sea   amasses.
Antidepressants, estrogen, cocaine.

oystercatcher, barnacle, crab, cutthroat eel

In the largest ocean, dead zones grow.
Run-off, slough-off, bleed-off
from factories, mills, mines.
Arsenic, lead, mercury, cyanide.

mussels, sea star, anemone, clam

Eelgrass meadows and kelp forests fill
with black oil from back alley grease monkeys.
Beached containers, abandoned boats leak
battery acid, jet fuel, radioactive waste.

flathead flounder, blackfin bass, sable fish

Farmers' fields, urban lawns, orchards
hoard ammonium nitrate, nitrous oxide.
Fertilizer and pesticide leach into stream,
river, estuary, become ocean, become. . . .

Alison Stone

The Sea

Storm-battered, the sailors pray to the sea.
The child's doll swept away by the sea.

Sun-drugged, I sleep heavily in Newport,
skin and hair sticky with spray from the sea.

The insane poor chained in windowless rooms.
For the rich—a holiday by the sea.

Poets, beware of mirrors, lovers' eyes,
the moon. And that soggy cliché, the sea.

Yesterday the despot stripped protection
from hibernating bears. Today, the sea.

Decades in a factory. If only
he'd been bold enough to run away to sea.

The young widow likes her men dangerous,
her whiskey neat, her underthings lacy.

Landlocked, the prisoner recited lists
of words like prayer—river, ship, bay, sea.

Dusk. The scavenging gulls blur to blobs. No
horizon line. Gray sky blends with gray sea.

After the clapping game and holiday
story, the preschoolers sculpt a clay C.

Boat ride with radio. Is my nausea
caused by the news or the sway of the sea?

The park littered with condoms. Food scraps turn
to compost. Lost divers decay in the sea.

Americans seem chained to Plato's cave
of illusions. Coming our way, the sea.

Walk on sand, Alison, let the waves take
your grief. Let go, they say. Obey the sea.

Leah Mueller

At the Memorial

Afraid to weep, my son carries
his father's ashes in a cardboard box.
As water roils in the distance,
he steps inside a crater filled with loose gravel,
twists his ankle, crumples to the ground.

We stand above, hands outstretched
while he tosses in agony on the asphalt.
On the shore, beachcombers
climb dead tree branches,
pick their way through slippery rocks.

My son's right knee ripped and swollen,
a jagged hole in his expensive pant leg.

I remember the other times he fell,
how I failed to offer comfort,
how he refused to cry
unless he had an injury.
How terrified he was of pain.
How he worked to clutch his intestines
tight, like a box, to keep it all inside.

The only way he mourns
is through his body:

he writhes and moans,
grief rising into the air like ashes.

"I'll be okay," he says,
lifting the box high, continuing
towards the water. A minute later,
I hold my jacket open to block the wind.
My daughter steps inside the folds,
lights a clump of sage with trembling hands.

Maybe we'll all meet somewhere,
but I'm inclined to doubt it.
I've been disappointed before,
gone to that ledge and found it empty.

In the distance, children leap across rocks,
their voices rising with the waves.

We each take a fistful of ashes,
toss them into the low tide.
Tiny crabs search our soles for food.

I clutch the dust of a man I quit
holding years ago, but finally release,
and return to my car without stumbling.

He left with no forwarding address,
dead finger pointing on the envelope,
mail piled on the floor of his

tiny, subsidized apartment.
Another person sleeps
in the bedroom where he died;
she's happy for the refuge.

All we know is shelter, then
someone who remains standing
long enough to let us go.

Meg Smith

Seafoam Witch

What we have raised,
from the cast
of driftwood,
spark to spark,
in the crush
of the wave—
what we have prayed,
scrit in the sand,
our fingers will cross,
and the gray green froth
will yet speak
what we've become.

Marj Hahne

Hold Fast

> after Jill Powers' *Holdfast: Seaweeds in a Time
> of Oceanic Change*, Dairy Arts Center,
> Boulder, CO, March 4-April 3, 2016

Start with a boat. Even if
it hangs from the sky.
Even if it's a floating
dream and the water's
breaking below. You are
alone again in the evening.
Something about a silver ring
you didn't see in the fog.
Start with fog, then,
lifting. Every morning
you don't wake up
in San Francisco.
In Colorado,
you are landlocked.
You hydrate your mood
in its predictable shifting:
Tide. Ebb and flood. Current.
You want to be anchored
here. Vascularly. Anatomically.
You've been waiting forty seasons
for your sister, for an oceanic love.
Last week, seaweed appeared
in a waking dream. Waving.
Fingering the bottom of your paper
canoe. Wanting to cling

to something moving and not
moving at the same time.
So, start with a boat in fog.
Or a tossed stone. Or the abandoned
shell of a mollusk. Let your heart swell
like an underwater forest, swaying
hello, goodbye, hello.

Clarissa Jakobsons

California Ohms

Are you alone, empty this June,
      feet tangled in your private dingy,
laying back on a sofa chair?
      Close your eyes, soak the sun
through these cracked window panes.
      Open the door, catch the breeze,
watch the western bluebird
      balance on a withered fence
as the succulent cactus lost a leaf.

Even moss ridden barnacles
      attach to driftwood planks
with longing. Sunset faces sparkle energy
      that dances with ferns breaking sky.
Sweet surrender. The Pacific speaks,
      each wave clear, but distinct
with gratitude for each passing seal
      or killer whale.

Next door, the weathervane turns
      unsure of direction as my toes
grip earth with ohms. Silence captures
      a West Port sunset,
the ancient cypress oversees all.

Gene Hult

Seizure

It will be told the rivers
shall swell with rust and vermin
through underground tunnels straining
to bear the solvent waters
and lessen in familiar grace.

Over bones a cycle of weeds
yellow flowers and pollen collectors
grand as inflated hippopotamuses
in spiky fields undulating with worms.

The birds flightless again, striding
to peck and flap at outsized insects,
pull each other apart in screeching
that signals how unsafe the night.

Where are we? Out on the salty
oceans, on pontoon islands, canoes
and yachts hooked together to surf
the storms, ricocheting
from uninhabitable coast
to toxic beach, following
the angry, fluctuating jetstream,
chanting prayers to sea gods
into the boiling morning sun.

We are already adapting,
salty babies crawling along ropes

and gangplanks, befriending the sea
mammals, adjusting to a diet of kelp
and krill, telling terrifying stories
of the glass canyons of man,
the creeping poison of our mistrust
and the flood promised never to return.

Power has reverted to matriarchy,
sea witches healing and midwifing
and auguring the weather,
influencing the direction
of the wind and breeding
of family stock.

Gestation slowed to incubate
to specification, but redundancy
foments scorn by generation, compliances
of drones, peaceful as rainwater brooks
but quieter, less tendency to overrun.

Codified standards of fact, policies
and amendments to truth decided
by representational committees of stern
traditionalists and calcified academics,
quick checklists of honesty,
no lies but narrow avenues
of ambiguity rarely allowed.

Religions dampened to outlaw sects,
sex projected in few combinations,
physical pleasure matter-of-fact as eating was.

A certain safety valve of rebellion
and expression allowed to churn
in certain submerged centers,
children with talent and anger
separated and inserted into enclaves
of opposition and artistic endeavor,
factories of entertainment and inspiration,
enough to kindle a reduced vanguard
of progression, as an unevolving
organism is soon extinct.

Those with scientific aptitude
are similarly sequestered on buoys,
given education and equipment to stir
the advancement of invention,
but without fame or privatization,
destructive impulses culled
for the safety of the sphere, for
common interest, with corruption
delegated to the accused accursed.

What engenders improvement, motivates
competition, enlivens ambition,
those forces of humanity that must
be addressed before they curdle into
dissatisfaction, languor, insurrection,
how to manifest incentive when
everyone has equal comfort and
access to their destined birthright.
Why do we get up in the morning,
what urges us to come and try,
what justifies and assigns purpose.

Why strive in a system of oppressive
yet comfortable equality afloat.

No fairy tale significance to opiate
and distract from suffering, no
chemical solace of serotonin uptake,
so what brings meaning to the passage
of time in its tedious but brief floating span.

Is it a lottery of love, a bribe
of romance, or simply a satisfaction
of achievement in an existence
provided with plenty but grinding
the many under a yoke of work
and mental oppression at sea.

We finally harnessed our strangest
intrinsic attribute, and elevated altruism
to fetishized pledged mottos of intent.

Dogs, cats, rats are with us,
roaches and beetles, spiders
and lizards, sea lions, and octopuses
clinging to the trailing lines like
waterskiers, twirling in kaleidoscope
colors to obscure the edges of our ecosystem.

The land is salted, bracken, blistered,
and although the grass grows ever taller,
it all belongs to the bees and worms.

Stephen McGuinness

Parallel

I keep the sea, always,
To left or right of me
Because easy roads,
Worth travelling, run
Parallel to shore.

I stop, turn, gaze out
Across blue-green water,
Raise a hand to worn,
Knotted, unseeing sailors,
My nails scraping gently on glass.

I leave in the lull
Between gusts, when
Fear overtakes wonder,
And salt spray drenches
My finely wrought clothes,

Moving out of range
As wild waves smash
Against quay walls, break on
Bleak black rocks and grind
Soft silver grains to sand.

Eloise Bruce

Having Uncles Named Homer

Shrimp, meaning "small"
and for the fisherman
of Cortez Village,
a livelihood.

For my little brother
after brain damage,
brain food. He ate
as many as he could stuff in his mouth.

They called from the Gulf of Mexico,
these noisy pink swirls,
they were; they still are, louder
than whales singing, dolphins
talking in the deep water,
as sexual as bats in air, who
might suck your juicy insides.

Those old days of segregation, we
went to Morrison's Cafeteria
and my Uncle Homer paid the check
for livelihood and brain food, all
you could eat, for all of us
and the sea chattered and told our secrets.

We grew and healed, we learned
to fly at night, live on land, drink.

We told the small secrets until they grew large,
until they flew inches above our heads,
until there were no secrets
and we didn't need our eyes to know

that shrimp screaming in water
is the loudest sound in the world.

Marjorie Maddox

Sea Side Be

Salt seasons all,
sautés our other lives out,
sun-grills sandy leisure
into each strand of hair,
each sea-stained square
of skin stretched tightly
toward that ungainly octopus
of sun. Listen. The tide's wet breath
wants only you. Let be.

Alec Solomita

Another Poem about the Sea

I.
Probably a bad idea to write
about the sea
but it's hard to resist when it's
breathing outside my
window and I'm at The Sandpiper
and the people
in the next room emerge to reveal a
family of three,
a young balding white guy, apologetically tall,
with a diminutive wife
and a serene baby
who sits in the crook of his dad's arm
resting his big
one-year-old head
on the man's scapula.

II.
So, last night I went outside at dusk
and a path of moonlight appeared
on the water, growing more distinct as dark came.

It was a waxing high yellow moon
and the path on the black water
was wide and modest.

Winston Plowes

Orcadian

The tide went out without saying goodbye
as you searched for yourself
under every petal of the night garden.

Looking for order in the random placement
of shells on an apron of grey pebbles.

Limpets, Pink Tellins, False Angel Wings.

A stowaway from the seaweed fields,
your dark hair anchored to a head of riches.
Teaching the fish to sing harmonies
fifty fathoms below
in the filtered light of a jetsam moon.

About the Authors

Dante Alighieri (1265-1321), often referred to simply as Dante, is widely considered the greatest Italian poet. His vision of the afterlife, *Divine Comedy*, is perhaps the preeminent poem of the Middle Ages, forming a foundation for Italy's literature, and fundamentally influencing Western civilization. His other works include *Convivio*, *La Vita Nuova*, and *De vulgari eloquentia*. **27**

Joel Allegretti is the author of, most recently, *Platypus* (NYQ Books, 2017), a collection of poems, prose, and performance texts, and *Our Dolphin* (Thrice Publishing, 2016), a novella. His second book of poems, *Father Silicon* (The Poet's Press, 2006), was selected by *The Kansas City Star* as one of 100 Noteworthy Books of 2006. He is the editor of *Rabbit Ears: TV Poems* (NYQ Books, 2015), the first anthology of poetry about the mass medium. Allegretti has published his poems in *The New York Quarterly*, *Barrow Street*, *Smartish Pace*, *PANK*, and many other national journals, as well as in journals published in Canada, the United Kingdom, Belgium, and India. **79, 93**

Carol Alena Aronoff, Ph.D. is a psychologist, teacher, and poet. Her work has appeared in numerous journals and anthologies and has won several prizes. She was twice nominated for a Pushcart Prize. She has published a chapbook (*Cornsilk*) and five books of her poems and photographs: *The Nature of Music*, *Cornsilk*, *Her Soup Made the Moon Weep*, *Blessings from an Unseen World*, as well as *Dreaming Earth's Body* (with artist Betsie Miller-Kusz). A new chapbook, *Tapestry of Secrets*, and a full-length book of poetry, *The Gift of Not Finding: Poems for Meditation*, are forthcoming. Currently she resides in rural Hawaii. **78**

Joseph Auslander (1897-1965) was an American poet, anthologist, translator of poems, and novelist. Auslander was appointed the first Poet Laureate Consultant in Poetry to the Library of Congress in 1937. Auslander's best-known work is *The Unconquerables*, a collection of poems addressed to the German-occupied countries of Europe. He served as the poetry editor for the *North American Review* and *The Measure*, and received the Robert Frost Prize for Poetry. **11**

Janet Barry is a musician, poet, and photographer, with poems published in numerous journals and anthologies, most recently *Snapdragon*, *Third Wednesday*, *Clementine*, and *Radius Lit*. Her photography has appeared in publications such as *Off the Coast*, *Around Concord*, and *Parenthesis*, and she has received several Pushcart nominations as well as a Best of the Net award from Bi Lines. Janet hold degrees in organ performance and poetry. **80**

Thomas Lovell Beddoes (1803-1849) was an English poet, dramatist, and physician. His *Death's Jest Book* and *Collected Poems* were published posthumously. **34**

Sidney Bending is a retired graphic artist living on an island off the west coast of Canada. Her award-winning poetry and flash fiction has been published in literary journals and anthologies in North America, the UK, India, Africa, and New Zealand. She is a member of Haiku Canada and the Haiku Society of America. Her first book of poetry, *Harmony Leaps*, a collaboration with Margaret Rutley, is printed in 2019 and available from Amazon.com. **101**

Ben Bever is a composition instructor at the Northern Virginia Community College, with a BA from Allegheny College in Pennsylvania and an MFA in Creative Writing from George Mason University in Virginia. He has lived in India, Pakistan, Indonesia, and Israel, and traveled to parts of Europe and Africa as well. His work has been published in *Willows Wept*, *Sixfold*, and the *Poets Are Present* anthology published by the Washington, DC Shakespeare Theatre. **75**

Jenny Blackford lives in Newcastle, Australia. Her poems and stories have appeared in *Australian Poetry Journal*, *Westerly*, *The Pedestal Magazine*, and more. Her poetry prizes include first place in the Thunderbolt Prize for Crime Poetry 2017, the Connemara Mussel Festival Poetry Competition 2016, the Humorous Verse section of the Henry Lawson awards in 2014 and 2017, and third in the ACU

Prize for Literature 2014. Much-awarded Sydney press Pitt Street Poetry published an illustrated pamphlet of her cat poems, *The Duties of a Cat*, in 2013, and her first full-length book of poetry, *The Loyalty of Chickens*, in 2017. **73**

Elizabeth Barrett Browning (1806-1861) was a popular and prolific English poet and abolitionist of the Victorian era, and was a rival to Alfred, Lord Tennyson as a candidate for poet laureate on the death of Wordsworth. She influenced Edgar Allen Poe, Emily Dickinson, Virginia Woolf, and Susan B. Anthony, among many others. **22, 65**

Eloise Bruce's book of poetry *Rattle* was published by CavenKerry Press. Over the years, she has had various roles at the Frost Place Center for Poetry and the Arts in Franconia, NH, and is the Youth Editor for *The RavensPerch*. She is a member of the poetry critique and performance group Cool Women and works as a teaching artist for Young Audiences of NJ and Eastern PA and Writer's Theatre of NJ. Please visit coolwomenpoets.org and cavankerrypress.org. **116**

George Shepard Burleigh (1821-1903) was a poet from a farm family in Plainfield, CT known for his anti-slavery writing and lecturing. His books include *Elegiac Poem on the Death of Nathaniel Peabody Rogers* and *The Maniac and Other Poems*. **35**

Lord Byron (1788-1824) was a notorious and charismatic English politician and poet of enduring fame. Formally named George Gordon Byron, 6th Baron Byron FRS, he is regarded as a prime member of the Romantic movement, and remains influential. His major works include *Don Juan*, *Darkness*, and *Childe Harold's Pilgrimage*. **53**

Bliss Carman (1861-1929) was a Canadian poet and essayist from New Brunswick who spent most of his life in the United States, particularly New York and Connecticut. Carman's metered, formal verse explores natural and spiritual themes. He is the author of more than 50 volumes of poetry, including *Low Tide on Grand Pré*, *Over the Wintry Threshold*, and *Later Poems*. **63**

R. T. Castleberry is a Pushcart Prize nominee and an internationally published poet. He was a co-founder of the Flying Dutchman Writers Troupe, co-editor/publisher of the poetry magazine *Curbside Review*, and an assistant editor for *Lily Poetry Review* and *Ardent*. His work has appeared in *The Alembic*, *Santa Fe Literary Review*, *Comstock Review*, *Roanoke Review*, *Pacific Review*, *Iodine*, *Foliate Oak*, and *Silk Road*. His chapbook *Arriving At The Riverside* was published by Finishing Line Press in January, 2010. An e-book, *Dialogue and Appetite*, was published by Right Hand Pointing in May, 2011. **95**

Stephen Crane (1871-1900) was a prolific American writer who won international acclaim for his Civil War novel *The Red Badge of Courage*. He became known for his writing in the Realist tradition, but also pioneered work as an Impressionist and Naturalist. He was an early, unconventional practitioner of free verse, seen in his poetry collections *War is Kind* and *The Black Riders and Other Lines*. **25**

Bill Cushing has lived in several states as well as the Virgin Islands and Puerto Rico. A creative writing and literature major at the University of Central Florida, Bill was named one of the "Top Los Angeles Poets for 2017" as well as honored among "Ten Poets to Watch in 2018." He has poems published in numerous print and online journals, and several anthologies, including the award-winning *Stories of Music*. Besides facilitating a writing workshop for 9 Bridges, Bill collaborates on the creative project "Notes and Letters," found at youtube.com/channel/UCcBq6xyF20DFZNuqaM_1x6Q and facebook.com/groups/100185423723709. **96**

H. D. (1886-1961) was an American poet, novelist, and memoirist named Hilda Doolittle, known as an avant-garde Imagist. Her poetry was often inspired by Greek mythology and classical poets. She was unapologetic about her sexuality and questioning of gender roles, and thus became an icon for both the LGBT rights and feminist movement. H. D. published numerous books of poetry, including *Flowering of the Rod*, *Red Roses From Bronze*, *Hymen*, and the posthumous *Helen in Egypt*. **10**

Lauren Davis is the author of the chapbook *Each Wild Thing's Consent* (Poetry Wolf Press). She holds an MFA from the

Bennington Writing Seminars, and her poetry and essays can be found in publications such as *Prairie Schooner*, *Spillway*, *Empty Mirror*, and *Lunch Ticket*. Davis teaches at The Writers' Workshoppe in Port Townsend, WA, and she works as an editor at *The Tishman Review*. **98**

Elizabeth Ruth Deyro is a poet, lifestyle journalist, and independent publisher based in the Philippines. Her work has been published in *Rust + Moth*, *Hypertrophic Literary*, *Half Mystic*, and *Philippines Graphic*; anthologized in *Beyond the Shallows* (L'Ephemere Review, 2018) and *The Anatomy of Desire* (The Poetry Annals, 2018); profiled in *Luna Luna Magazine* and *Maudlin House*; adapted into film and exhibited in House of Frida (Bacolod City, 2019) and Cinema Centenario (Quezon City, 2019); and nominated for the Pushcart Prize. She is the curator of *RECLAIM: An Anthology of Women's Poetry*, founder of *The Brown Orient*, and a writer at *Philippine Tatler*. **82**

Emily Dickinson (1830-1886) was American lyric poet who lived mostly in isolation with her family in Amherst, MA, and commanded an original brilliance of style and integrity of vision. Her poetry was not publicly recognized in her lifetime, but she is now considered to be one of the most important and influential 19th-century American poets and a central figure in Western literature. **19, 49, 60**

A. E. (1867-1935) is the poetic pseudonym of George William Russell, an Irish writer, publisher, painter, and politician from Dublin. A lifelong friend of William Butler Yeats, he also often wrote on mystical themes. His books include *Homeward: Songs by the Way*, *By Still Waters*, and *Song and Its Fountains*. **20**

Ralph Waldo Emerson (1803-1882) was a challenging and intellectually influential American writer and lecturer from Massachusetts known as the leader of the Transcendentalists, who championed individualism, insight, and the unity of all creation. His best known poems include "Concord Hymn," "The Rhodora," "Brahma," and "Uriel." **36**

Agnieszka Filipek lives in Galway, Ireland. She writes in both her native tongue Polish and in English, and also translates in these languages. Her work was published internationally in countries such as Poland, Ireland, India, China, England, Wales, Germany, Bangladesh, Canada, and the United States. Recently her poems appeared in *Marble Poetry Magazine, Halcyon Days, Light Journal, Bonsai Journal, The Stony Thursday Book, Balloons Literary Journal*, and *The Writers' Cafe Magazine*. For more see agnieszkafilipek.com. **99**

Charlotte Perkins Gilman (1860-1935) was an esteemed American writer from Connecticut. After moving to California, she became a lecturer for social reform as a utopian feminist, championing women's economic autonomy. Perhaps her best known work is her semi-autobiographical short story "The Yellow Wallpaper," inspired by her experience with extreme postpartum psychiatric difficulties. Her poetry collections include *In This Our World* and *Suffrage Songs and Verses*. **46**

Arthur Guiterman (1871-1943) was an American poet, editor, and librettist known for his humor. He cofounded the Poetry Society of America. His poetry collections include *The Laughing Muse, Wildwood Fables*, and *Brave Laughter*. **59**

Marj Hahne is a freelance editor and writing teacher, and a 2015 MFA graduate from the Rainier Writing Workshop, with a concentration in poetry. She has performed and taught at more than 100 venues around the country, as well as been featured on public radio and television programs. Her poems have appeared in literary journals, anthologies, art exhibits, and dance performances. Please visit MarjHahne.com. **108**

Thomas Hardy (1840-1928) was an English novelist and poet of the Victorian era, straddling both Realism and Romanticism. While Hardy regarded himself primarily as a poet, initially he gained renown as the novelist of *Far from the Madding Crowd, Tess of the d'Urbervilles*, and *Jude the Obscure*. His poetry collections include *Satires of Circumstance, Moments of Vision*, and *Winter Words in Various Moods and Metres*. **14**

Sadakichi Hartmann (1867-1944) was a critic of American art and photography, and a modernist poet of German and Japanese heritage. His poetry, influenced by the Symbolists as well as haiku, includes *Drifting Flowers of the Sea and Other Poems*, *My Rubaiyat*, and *Japanese Rhythms*. **8**

Nathaniel Hawthorne (1804-1864) is considered one of the greatest American novelists. His themes often center on the inherent evil and sin of humanity, and his works often have moral messages and deep psychological complexity. His published works include *The Scarlet Letter*, *The House of Seven Gables*, and *Twice-Told Tales*. **51**

David Holper has done a little bit of everything: taxi driver, fisherman, dishwasher, bus driver, soldier, house painter, bike mechanic, bike courier, and teacher. He has published a number of stories and poems, including two collections of poetry: *The Bridge* (Sequoia Song Publications) and *64 Questions* (March Street Press). His poems have appeared in numerous literary journals and anthologies, and he has recently won several poetry competitions, in spite of his contention that he never wins anything. He teaches English at College of the Redwoods and lives in Eureka, CA, far enough the madness of civilization that he can still see the stars at night and hear the Canada geese calling. **76**

Gene Hult is the publisher of Houston, TX-based Brighten Press, and edited this anthology. After being the managing editor of the *Denver Quarterly*, he worked in children's editorial in NYC for nearly 30 years. Gene has written more than 120 books published for children and young adults, mostly under his pseudonym J. E. Bright (jebright.com). His first book of poetry was entitled *Render*, and his second, *Catfish and After*, is forthcoming in 2019. Please visit genehult.com, or follow Gene on Twitter and Instagram @citysqwirl. **83, 111**

Clarissa Jakobsons, Aurora, OH, teaches art and writing courses at a local community college. Her art work has been widely exhibited. She enjoyed a Provincetown Fine Arts Work Center artist residency and is currently working on a book of poems. Visiting Cape Cod during her college years instilled a love for the ocean without knowing why it felt like home. When her daughters visited

Lithuania and sent photos of the Baltic dunes, she understood the connection—the sea harbors a special place in her family's DNA. Clarissa curls toes in sand listening to the ocean's heartbeat, as if it was her own. **110**

Thomas S. Jones, Jr. (1882-1932) was a New York poet interested in lucid suggestion, subtle simplicity, and delicate lyricism. He was on the dramatic staff of the *New York Times*. His poetry collections include *Path of Dreams*, *Interludes*, *The Voice in the Silence*, and *The Rose-Jar*. **61**

Rudyard Kipling (1865-1936) was a popular English writer whose childhood in India informs his work. Among his novels and books of stories are *The Jungle Book*, *Just So Stories for Little Children*, and *Kim*. His poetry collections include *The Seven Seas*, *The Years Between*, and *The Muse Among the Motors*. He was the first English-language writer to be awarded the Nobel Prize in Literature. **17**

D. H. Lawrence (1885-1930) was a controversial English writer who delved into themes of sexuality and sensuality, modernity and industrialization, and human instinct. Among his popular books are the novels *Sons and Lovers*, *Women in Love*, and *Lady Chatterley's Lover*; and the short story collection *The Prussian Officer and Other Stories*. His poetry collections include *Birds, Beasts and Flowers*; *Pansies*; and *The Triumph of the Machine*. **58**

Eugene Lee-Hamilton (1845-1907) was an English poet and novelist particularly recognized for his formal craftsmanship and supernatural fiction. The Eugene Lee-Hamilton Poetry Competition for best Petrarchan sonnet by an undergraduate student at Oxford or Cambridge has been held since 1943. His books include *Sonnets of the Wingless Hours*, *Mimma Bella*, and *The Lord of the Dark Red Star*. **3**

Henry Wadsworth Longfellow (1807-1882), born in Portland, ME, was the most popular American poet of his time, known for his lyric verse about legends and myths. Among his most celebrated poems are "Paul Revere's Ride," "The Song of Hiawatha," and "Evangeline." He was the first American to translate Dante

Alighieri's *Divine Comedy*. His poetry collections include *Voices of the Night*, *The Seaside and the Fireside*, and *The Masque of Pandora and Other Poems*. **32**

Marjorie Maddox, a professor of English and Creative Writing at Lock Haven University, has published 11 collections of poetry—including *True, False, None of the Above* (Poiema Poetry Series, Illumination Book Award Medalist); *Local News from Someplace Else*; *Wives' Tales*; *Transplant, Transport, Transubstantiation* (2004 Yellowglen Prize; re-release 2018); *Perpendicular As I* (Sandstone Book Award); the short story collection *What She Was Saying* (Fomite Press); 4 children's books; *Common Wealth: Contemporary Poets on Pennsylvania* (co-editor); *Presence* (assistant editor); and more than 550 stories, essays, and poems in journals and anthologies. For more information, please see marjoriemaddox.com. **118**

Paul Magrs is the author of many books, written for all ages and in many different genres, including *The Brenda and Effie Mysteries* and numerous *Doctor Who* novels, radio plays, and short stories. His book on writing and creativity, *The Novel Inside You*, is published by Snowbooks. He taught novel writing in the MA program in Creative Writing at UEA, and then at Manchester Metropolitan. Paul lives in Manchester, England, with his partner, Jeremy, and is now a full-time writer. **85**

Lucinda Marshall is a writer, artist, and activist. Her poetry publications include *Sediments*, *GFT*, *Tuck Magazine*, *Stepping Stones Magazine*, *Columbia Journal*, *Poetica*, *Haikuniverse*, *ISLE*, and her work appears in the anthologies *Poems in the Aftermath* (Indolent Books) and *We Will Not Be Silenced* (Indie Blu(e) Publishing). Lucinda is the founder and host of the DiVerse Gaithersburg Poetry Reading and Open Mic. She cares deeply about ocean ecology and hopes to live under the sea in her next life. Please visit her website at lucindamarshall.com. **91**

John Masefield (1878-1967) was a prolific English writer and playwright who had popular novels, poetry, children's books, non-fiction, and autobiographies published. He was the UK Poet Laureate from 1930 to 1967. His poetry collections include *Salt-Water Ballads*, *The Daffodil Fields*, and *Reynard the Fox*. **13**

Stephen McGuinness lives in Ireland and writes poetry and occasional short stories, some of which gets published in journals. **115**

Edna St. Vincent Millay (1892-1950) was an American poet and playwright. She wrote verse plays early in her career, and was commissioned by the Metropolitan Opera House to write a libretto for a successful opera composed by Deems Taylor called *The King's Henchman*. Millay received the Pulitzer Prize for Poetry in 1923, the third woman to win the award, and was also known for her feminist activism and as an icon of the LGBTQ community. Her poetry books include *Renascence, Second April,* and *The Murder of Lidice*. **9, 68**

Thomas Moore (1779-1852) was an Irish poet, singer, songwriter, and entertainer. He wrote lyrics to a series of folk tunes, and his *Irish Melodies* became extremely popular, particularly songs such as "The Minstrel Boy," "The Last Rose of Summer," and "Oft in the Stilly Night." His *Melodies* were not gathered into a collected volume until after his death. As Lord Byron's named literary executor, Moore was responsible for burning Lord Byron's memoirs. **26**

Marianne Moore (1887-1972) was an American modernist poet, critic, translator, editor, and suffragist. Her work is noted for wittiness, a satirical flair, precision, and technical innovation within formal verse. Her books include *The Pangolin and Other Verse, O to Be a Dragon,* and *The Accented Syllable*. In one of her most famous lines, she called for poetry to be created as "imaginary gardens with real toads in them." She won the Pulitzer Prize in Poetry. **4, 16**

Leah Mueller is an indie writer and spoken word performer from Tacoma, WA. She is the author of two chapbooks and four books. Her latest book, a memoir entitled *Bastard of a Poet* was published by Alien Buddha Press in June 2018. Leah's work appears or is forthcoming in *Blunderbuss, The Spectacle, Outlook Springs, Mojave River Review, Drunk Monkeys, Atticus Review, Your Impossible Voice, Wolfpack Press*, and other publications. She was a featured poet at the 2015 New York Poetry Festival, and a runner-up in the 2012 Wergle Flomp humor poetry contest. **104**

Eva L. Ogden (1853-1919) lived in a home called Lilacstead in Wilton, CT, and had poems and short stories appear in *The Century Magazine*, *St. Nicholas Magazine*, and *Harper's Magazine*, among other publications. Her books include *Did Ye Hear?* (illustrated by H. G. Thomson), *Along the Highways and Byways of Wilton*, and *Christmas Legends*. **67**

John Boyle O'Reilly (1844-1890) was an Irish-American writer and activist. Early on, he joined the Fenians, also known as Irish Republican Brotherhood, which got him transported to Australia. After escaping to the United States, he became a prominent spokesperson for the Irish community and culture, through his editorship of the Boston newspaper *The Pilot*, his prolific writing, and his lecture tours. His published works include *Songs from the Southern Seas*, *In Bohemia*, and *Watchwords*. **38**

Ciarán Parkes lives in Galway, Ireland, where he enjoys taking photographs and swimming in the cold Atlantic. His poems have been published in *The Rialto*, *Poetry Ireland Review*, *The Threepenny Review*, and other places. He also writes song lyrics for the Galway band This Lunar Mansion. Some photos can be found at instagram.com/ciaran9. **97**

Winston Plowes shares his floating home in Calderdale, UK with his 17-year-old cat, Sausage. He teaches Creative Writing in schools and to local groups while she dreams of Mouseland. His latest collection *Tales from the Tachograph* was published jointly with Gaia Holmes in 2018 by Calder Valley Poetry. Please visit winstonplowes.co.uk. **120**

Ezra Pound (1885-1972) was an American poet and critic, known for defining and popularizing the Imagism and Modernism poetry movements. A fierce advocate for other writers, he helped further the careers of Robert Frost, T. S. Eliot, Marianne Moore, H. D., James Joyce, W. B. Yeats, and William Carlos Williams. His books of poetry include *Exultations*, *Personae*, and *The Cantos*. **5**

Suzanne S. Rancourt, of Abenaki/Huron decent, is a multi-modal Expressive Arts Therapist and CASAC with degrees in Psychology and Creative Writing. Her book of poetry *Billboard in the Clouds* received the Native Writers' Circle of the Americas First Book Award. Her second is *murmurs at the gate* (Unsolicited Press, 2019). Ms. Rancourt's work has appeared in *Tiny Flames Press, Big Pond Rumours, Quiddity, River Heron Review, Shaking the Sheets, The Gyroscope Review, Young Ravens Literary Review, Tupelo Press Native Voices Anthology, Bright Hill Press 25th Anniversary Anthology, Slipstream, Muddy River Poetry Review, Ginosko, Journal of Military Experience, Cimarron Review,* and *Callaloo.* Ms. Rancourt is a USMC and Army veteran. **89**

Rainer Maria Rilke (1875-1926) was a Bohemian-Austrian writer who remains consistently popular and oft-quoted. His mystical, existential themes and intense lyricism lead him to be critically considered a transitional figure into Modernism. His collections of poetry include *Life and Songs, The Book of Hours,* and *Duino Elegies.* A book of his inspirational correspondence, *Letters to a Young Poet,* has influenced generations of artists. **50**

Dante Gabriel Rossetti (1828-1882) was a British poet, artist, and translator, known for his sensual themes and medieval revivalism. He founded the Pre-Raphaelite Brotherhood, and influenced the European Symbolists and the Aesthetic movement. He frequently wrote sonnets to accompany his pictures, while also creating art to illustrate books such as *Goblin Market and Other Poems* written by his sister Christina Rossetti. His many books combining writing and art include *Beauty and the Bird, Hand and Soul,* and *A Sea-Spell.* **56**

Alan Seeger (1888-1916) was an American bohemian poet from New York, best known for the poem "I Have a Rendezvous with Death," beloved by President John F. Kennedy. Seeger joined the French Foreign Legion during World War I, and died in the Battle of the Somme. The French honored him and other American soldiers with a statue in Paris, the base of which was inscribed with excerpts from his poem "Ode in Memory of the American Volunteers Fallen for France." His poetry collection is entitled *Poems.* **7**

William Shakespeare (1564-1616) is widely regarded as the greatest writer in the English language and the world's greatest dramatist.

His plays have been translated into every major living language and are performed more often than those of any other playwright. Shakespeare's 154 heartfelt *Sonnets*, profound meditations on the nature of love, sexual passion, procreation, death, and time, were published in 1609. **21**

Meg Smith is a poet, journalist, dancer, and events producer living in Lowell, MA. Her poetry has appeared in *The Blue Hour Anthology*, *The Cafe Review*, *Poetry Bay*, *Raven Cage eZine*, *Bewildering Stories*, and more. She is a past member of the board of Lowell Celebrates Kerouac!, a festival dedicated to the Lowell-born author. Her most recent poetry books, *Dear Deepest Ghost* and *This Scarlet Dancing*, are available on Amazon. She welcomes visits at megsmithwriter.net. **107**

Alec Solomita has published fiction in *The Mississippi Review*, *Southwest Review*, *Heart of Flesh*, and *The Adirondack Review*, among other publications. He was shortlisted by the Bridport Prize and *Southword Journal*, and named a finalist by the *Noctua Review*. His poetry has appeared in *Algebra of Owls*, *Literary Orphans*, *The Galway Review*, *Driftwood Press*, and elsewhere. His poetry chapbook *Do Not Forsake Me* was published by Finishing Line Press in 2017, and was nominated for a Massachusetts Book Award. He lives in Somerville, MA. **92, 119**

John Sterling (1806-1844) was a Scottish author, born on the Isle of Bute. His works include a novel, *Arthur Coningsby*, two books of poetry, *Poems* and *Election, a Poem*, and a tragic play, *Strafford*. He had essays and short stories published in *Blackwood's Magazine*. His biography, *The Life of John Sterling*, was written by Thomas Carlyle. **62**

Wallace Stevens (1879-1955) was a respected and precise American Modernist poet, concerned with the intersection of imagination and reality. He was born in Reading, PA, and had a full career as an insurance company executive in Hartford, CT. He won the Pulitzer Prize for Poetry. His collections include *Harmonium*, *The Man with the Blue Guitar*, *Notes Toward a Supreme Fiction*, and *The Auroras of Autumn*. **12**

Robert Louis Stevenson (1850-1894) was an insightful writer of enduring popularity from Edinburgh, Scotland. He's renowned for his vivid, gothic novels *Treasure Island*, *Kidnapped*, and *Strange Case of Dr Jekyll and Mr Hyde*. His books of poetry include *A Child's Garden of Verses*, *Underwoods*, and *Songs of Travel and Other Verses*. **64**

Alison Stone has published six full-length collections: *Caught in the Myth* (NYQ Books, 2019), *Dazzle* (Jacar Press, 2017), *Masterplan*, a book of collaborative poems with Eric Greinke (Presa Press, 2018), *Ordinary Magic*, (NYQ Books, 2016), *Dangerous Enough* (Presa Press, 2014), and *They Sing at Midnight*, which won the 2003 Many Mountains Moving Poetry Award; as well as three chapbooks. Her poems have appeared in *The Paris Review*, *Poetry*, *Ploughshares*, *Barrow Street*, *Poet Lore*, and many other journals and anthologies. She has been awarded *Poetry*'s Frederick Bock Prize and *New York Quarterly*'s Madeline Sadin Award. She was recently Writer in Residence at LitSpace St. Pete. She is also a painter and the creator of *The Stone Tarot*. A licensed psychotherapist, she has private practices in NYC and Nyack. Please visit stonepoetry.org and stonetarot.com. **102**

Sara Teasdale (1884-1933) was an American lyric poet, known for her intense verse written in classical forms. Her book of poems, *Love Songs*, won the first Columbia Poetry Prize, which would be renamed the Pulitzer Prize for Poetry. Her other poetry collections include *Helen of Troy and Other Poems*, *Rivers to the Sea*, *Dark of the Moon*, and *Strange Victory*. **52**

Alfred, Lord Tennyson (1809-1892) was a British poet, exceptionally famous during his lifetime, adept at excellently-crafted lyric romantic melancholia with memorable visual imagery. He was the Poet Laureate of Great Britain and Ireland during much of Queen Victoria's reign. Among his works are *Poems, Chiefly Lyrical*; *In Memoriam*; and *Idylls of the King*. **30**

Larry D. Thacker's poetry is in more than 150 publications including *Spillway*, *Still: The Journal*, *Valparaiso Poetry Review*, *American Journal of Poetry*, *Poetry South*, *The Southern Poetry Anthology*, *Mojave River Review*, *The Lake*, *Illuminations Literary Magazine*, and

Appalachian Heritage. His books include *Mountain Mysteries*, and the poetry books *Drifting in Awe*, *Voice Hunting*, *Memory Train*, *Feasts of Evasion*, and *Grave Robber Confessional*. His MFA in poetry and fiction is earned from West Virginia Wesleyan College. Visit his website at larrydthacker.com. **100**

Lynne Viti is a lecturer emerita in the Writing Program, Wellesley College. She has published two chapbooks, *Baltimore Girls* (2017) and *The Glamorganshire Bible* (2018), from Finishing Line Press, and three micro-chapbooks: *Punting*, (2017), *Dreaming Must be Done in the Daytime* (2018), and *In Louisburgh, County Mayo* (2019), from Origami Poems Project. She blogs at stillinschool.wordpress.com. **87**

Walt Whitman (1819-1892) was one of the greatest and most influential American writers, often considered the progenitor of free verse. A Humanist and a believer in an interdependent responsibility between poet and society, he straddles the movements of Transcendentalism and Realism. His work includes the poetry books *Leaves of Grass* and *Drum-Taps*, and the essay collections *Manly Health and Training*, *Democratic Vistas*, and *Specimen Days & Collect*. **18**

Oscar Wilde (1854-1900) was a poet, novelist, essayist, and playwright from Dublin, Ireland, known for his clever comedic wit, humorous yet challenging philosophies, and controversial, flamboyant life. Raised and educated as a Classicist, he transitioned into the Aesthetic and Decadent movements, with complex and contradictory uses of Moralism. His enduringly popular plays include *Lady Windermere's Fan*, *A Woman of No Importance*, and *The Importance of Being Earnest*. His novel *The Picture of Dorian Gray* ranks with the best of Gothic fiction. His poems include *Ravenna*, *The Sphinx*, and *The Ballad of Reading Gaol*. **6**

William Wordsworth (1770-1850) was a major English poet. With Samuel Taylor Coleridge, he helped to launch the Romantic Age in English literature with their co-written *Lyrical Ballads*.

Wordsworth's masterwork is *The Recluse*, a semi-autobiographical poem started in his twenties but remained unfinished; the first and second sections were published as *The Prelude* (considered by itself his finest work) and *The Excursion*. Wordsworth was Britain's poet laureate from 1843 to his death. His other works include *Poems, in Two Volumes*; *The White Doe of Rylstone*; and *Laodamia*. **70**

William Butler Yeats (1865-1939) was an Irish poet and one of the great writers of the 20th century. A pillar of the Irish literary establishment, he helped to found the Abbey Theatre, and in his later years served two terms as a Senator of the Irish Free State. Often considered a Symbolist, he was preoccupied with metaphysics, the occult, physical and spiritual masks, mythology (especially Irish legends) as well as with cyclical theories of life, although he retained his formalism. He was awarded the Nobel Prize in Literature. His poetry collections include *The Wild Swans at Coole*, *The Tower*, and *The Winding Stair and Other Poems*. **24**

Acknowledgments

"Let The Oceans Speak For Me" by Elizabeth Ruth Deyro was first published by *Porridge Magazine* under the title "They hear my voice when the ocean speaks."

"At the Memorial" by Leah Mueller first appeared on *Elephants Never*.

"Land Not Required" by Lauren Davis first appeared in *Calliope*.

"Sailing" by Bill Cushing is included in his book *A Former Life* (Finishing Line Press).

"Sea Side Be" by Marjorie Maddox originally appeared in *Local News from Someplace Else* (Wipf and Stock).

"Sea Stack" by Gene Hult appeared in his book *Render* (Brighten Press).

"The Muse" by Carol Alena Aronoff first appeared in *Verse of Silence*.

"The Way the Water" by Jenny Blackford appeared in her collection *The Loyalty of Chickens* (Pitt Street Poetry).

"To Pewetole Island" by David Holper is included in his book *The Bridge* (Sequoia Song Publications).

"Lament" by Lynne Viti first appeared in *Stillwater Review*.

"The Sea at Our Door" by Joel Allegretti was first published in *River Oak Review*. "Gabriel the Beachcomber" appears in his collection *Father Silicon* (The Poet's Press).

"Kelp" by Ciarán Parkes won the Waterford Poetry Prize. It was later first published in *Coast to Coast to Coast*.

"The Mission of Water" by R. T. Castleberry originally appeared in *San Pedro River Review*.

"Having Uncles Named Homer" by Eloise Bruce appeared in her book *Rattle* (CavanKerry Press).

Reading Guide

1. Choose any ocean poem in this book, and read it to yourself with as much **attention** as you can muster. Don't be put off by poetic language or get annoyed if you get lost—stick with it to the end. Let the words wash through you without your experience of the poem being affected by expectations.

2. Read a poem **aloud**. Your grasp of it may change by listening to the music in the words, its cadences and rhythms. Do you find yourself savoring particular phrases as they roll off your tongue? Perhaps you may be reminded of a song, or the sounds will evoke sensory memories of the ocean.

3. When you first read a poem from the book, let go of the need for meaning or visuals, and simply feel the **emotion** in the words. You may get a rich sense of the poem by the moods it inspires alone.

4. Notice the **form** of a poem. Does it rhyme? Is it broken into stanzas? Is the poem narrative—does it tell a story—or is it abstract? Is it formal, with a patterned rhyme scheme, or free verse, where anything goes? Does the form detract from or accentuate your sense of the poem?

5. Consider the **vocabulary** of a poem. Are there words you don't know or can't figure out from context? Choose a word you aren't sure about and look it up. Is it an archaic, old-fashioned word, the name of a place, or a strange usage? Does learning the meaning change the poem in a noticeable way?

6. Look at a poem's **title**. Does your sense of the text match the heading? Is it ironic or clever, or some other kind of twist in significance? Would you title the poem differently?

7. Observe a poem's **imagery**. What do you see as you read? Are the verbal pictures unconnected fragments, or can you imagine a coherent scene? Ask yourself if the visual imagery is symbolic or realistic—does it represent or suggest more than itself (connote), or do the words merely indicate the literal object they describe (denote)?

8. Consider a poem's **figurative language**. Are there comparisons? Look for similes, which often use the words "like" or "as" to equate different things. Then look for metaphors, which also indicate connection between unlike things, but boldly identify those relationships as true. You may also spot oxymorons (paired contradictions), hyperbole (exaggeration on purpose), or personification (inanimate objects given human personality traits). What effects are achieved by these techniques?

9. What is the **situation** in a poem? Attempt to figure out the circumstances being described, although it's not always possible in abstract poetry. Is there a story, with action and events? Can you identify the setting, where and when it takes place? How does the situation relate to the ocean?

10. Are there **characters** in the poem? Is the poet a character? Maybe the speaker is not the writer but a fictionalized character. To whom is the poem addressed? Are you imagining yourself in the poem?

11. There may or may not be a specific **meaning** to a poem. Avoid the urge to paraphrase—to sum up in a sentence or two—rather than experience reading the poem as an integral event in time. The poem is not necessarily a puzzle to solve to receive a grand moral revelation. Allow it to quiet you or excite you with beauty, wisdom, or ambiguity as you read.

12. When discussing your experience of reading a poem, you share your **interpretation**. This is what you bring to the poem, based on your own interests, knowledge, history, and beliefs. Your take is as valid as any reader's. If you found a particular poem as a younger or older self, would you experience it differently? How about in a different mood?

13. Consider your **memories** that may surface. Are you reminded of moments involving the sea in your own life? What caused the memory to bubble up? How does it differ from what you read in a poem?

14. Read the **biography** blurb about the poet and then reread their poem. Does knowing more about the poet change your interpretation and enjoyment?

15. Read a classic poem and then a poem by a current writer and **compare** them. Are there stylistic changes you notice that have shifted over time? How does history affect your sense of each poem?

16. A great way to appreciate poetry is to **write** a poem. The memory prompts in question 13 are a good start. Be encouraged by the expression of these poets, but find inspiration in the first-hand source, your own perceptions and impressions of the ocean.

17. Poetry is not separate from the world. It can be **political**. People are part of the planetary ocean ecosystem. Who polluted the seas? Who owns them? How might changes in the ocean affect the economy and society? What can be done to restore the world's waters? Who should be responsible?

18. The poems in this book explore varied **aspects** of the ocean. What do you consider the most crucial component of the ocean, as a source of entertainment, food, inspiration, travel, weather, life, or beauty?

Brighten Press

The Power of Words to Enlighten and Entertain

With all the many other demands on your attention in the world, we appreciate you taking the time to read this book.

We welcome you to explore our growing list of poetry, humor, and children's book titles at **brightenpress.com**.

www.ingramcontent.com/pod-product-compliance
Lightning Source LLC
Chambersburg PA
CBHW030326080526
44584CB00012B/737